Cambridge Elements

Elements in Gender and Politics
edited by
Tiffany D. Barnes
University of Texas at Austin
Diana Z. O'Brien
Washington University in St. Louis

TOWARDS TOLERANCE AND ACCEPTANCE

Public Opinion and LGBTQ+ Politics in Latin America

Mariela Daby
Reed College

Eli G. Rau
Tecnologico de Monterrey

Shaftesbury Road, Cambridge CB2 8EA, United Kingdom

One Liberty Plaza, 20th Floor, New York, NY 10006, USA

477 Williamstown Road, Port Melbourne, VIC 3207, Australia

314–321, 3rd Floor, Plot 3, Splendor Forum, Jasola District Centre,
New Delhi – 110025, India

Cambridge University Press is part of Cambridge University Press & Assessment,
a department of the University of Cambridge.

We share the University's mission to contribute to society through the pursuit of
education, learning and research at the highest international levels of excellence.

www.cambridge.org
Information on this title: www.cambridge.org/9781009537407
DOI: 10.1017/9781009537445

© Mariela Daby and Eli G. Rau 2026

This publication is in copyright. Subject to statutory exception and to the provisions
of relevant collective licensing agreements, no reproduction of any part may take
place without the written permission of Cambridge University Press & Assessment.

When citing this work, please include a reference to the DOI 10.1017/9781009537445

First published 2026

A catalogue record for this publication is available from the British Library

A Cataloging-in-Publication data record for this Element is available from the Library
of Congress

ISBN 978-1-009-53740-7 Hardback
ISBN 978-1-009-53739-1 Paperback
ISSN 2753-8117 (online)
ISSN 2753-8109 (print)

Additional resources for this publication at www.cambridge.org/Rau

Cambridge University Press & Assessment has no responsibility for the persistence
or accuracy of URLs for external or third-party internet websites referred to in this
publication and does not guarantee that any content on such websites is, or will
remain, accurate or appropriate.

For EU product safety concerns, contact us at Calle de José Abascal, 56, 1°, 28003
Madrid, Spain, or email eugpsr@cambridge.org

Towards Tolerance and Acceptance

Public Opinion and LGBTQ+ Politics in Latin America

Elements in Gender and Politics

DOI: 10.1017/9781009537445
First published online: February 2026

Mariela Daby
Reed College

Eli G. Rau
Tecnologico de Monterrey

Author for correspondence: Mariela Daby, mariela@reed.edu

Abstract: Latin America has experienced an unprecedented expansion of LGBTQ+ rights in recent decades. Although obstacles remain for LGBTQ+ citizens, countries such as Uruguay and Argentina have become world leaders in enacting LGBTQ+ rights, and public opinion has shifted dramatically toward more positive sentiments. What underlies these shifting attitudes? Drawing on both survey data and interviews, we describe multiple processes by which individuals move from prejudice and rejection to tolerance and acceptance. We show that attitude change is often slow and gradual, and that explaining these trends requires attention to both macrolevel forces and individual experiences. In Latin America, a boom in international tourism created economic incentives for tolerance; broad shifts in demographics and the media landscape created openings for people to reconsider what a family looks like; and societies grappling with human rights abuses were more receptive to appeals for protecting LGBTQ+ rights as human rights.

Keywords: LGBTQ+, Latin America, same-sex marriage, trans rights, public opinion

© Mariela Daby and Eli G. Rau 2026

ISBNs: 9781009537407 (HB), 9781009537391 (PB), 9781009537445 (OC)
ISSNs: 2753-8117 (online), 2753-8109 (print)

Contents

1	Introduction	1
2	The Current Landscape of Public Opinion	7
3	How Does Attitude Change Happen?	21
4	When Friends and Family Come Out	24
5	Changing Behavior before Attitudes: Economic Incentives for Tolerance	34
6	Pop Culture and Representation	38
7	Demographic Changes and the Nuclear Family	43
8	Public Policy and LGBTQ+ Rights	53
9	Conclusions	69
	References	74

1 Introduction

From public opinion and social norms to legal recognition and public policy, the environment for LGBTQ+ populations in Latin America has changed dramatically in recent decades. A sea change in attitudes is evident in many arenas. Consider the transformation of pride events. The first pride march in Latin America was held in 1979 in Mexico (Encarnación 2016: 29). Pride marches began as countercultural events with few brave spectators. Historical and photographic records show how most of those in attendance at the first marches used masks to avoid being identified. Testimonies collected from the first pride marches suggest that most attendees were afraid of losing their employment if they were identified in pictures taken by the press for the newspapers (Bellucci 2010).

These early pride marches pushed back against respectability politics, and they were profoundly political. Carlos Jauregui, a renowned Argentine gay activist and founder of the *Comunidad Homosexual Argentina* (Argentine Homosexual Community) played a crucial role in promoting Argentina's first pride march (*marcha del orgullo*) in 1992. He envisioned organizing and attending the event as a political act: "In a society that educates us to be ashamed of ourselves, pride [or being proud] is a political response" (Bellucci 2010). To participate in pride was an act of courage and defiance.

Over time, the masks came off and gay pride marches spread throughout major metropolitan areas across the region. In 2009, São Paulo's pride march earned a spot in the Guinness Book of World Records for the largest pride march in history, with more than three million people in the crowds (Encarnación 2016: 30). As pride grew more mainstream, it also became commodified. One account of São Paulo's 2017 pride march described a barrage of corporate sponsorship, from rainbow-themed Burger King crowns to Doritos bags, the latter handed out by people wearing T-shirts displaying the tagline "There's nothing BOLDER than being yourself," a play on a common Doritos marketing slogan (Lamond 2018: 9–10).

The shift is stunning. A few decades ago, publicly participating in a pride event posed such a danger to one's reputation and livelihood that participants wore masks to maintain anonymity. Today, it is so mainstream that millions of people openly attend and major corporations have concluded that it is in their business interest to appear as a sponsor. How did public opinion and social attitudes change so dramatically? That is the question that we address in this Element.

Bringing together data from public opinion surveys and in-depth interviews, we show that these societal shifts toward tolerance and acceptance stem from individual-level attitude change. It is not simply driven by a dynamic of generational replacement, where each generation is more accepting than the last. Rather, many individuals gradually shift their perspective over time. These individual-level shifts happen slowly, and the sources of attitude change are varied. But across a diverse set of mechanisms for change, one unifying feature is the humanization of LGBTQ+ people that fosters empathy.[1]

One of the most powerful forms of this dynamic arises when friends and family members come out. For those holding negative attitudes toward LGBTQ+ communities, the revelation that someone they love and admire belongs to these communities can force them to reconsider their assumptions. And when they change their attitudes toward their LGBTQ+ loved ones, they often begin to change their broader attitudes about LGBTQ+ rights.

These changes happen slowly and often in stages. Throughout this Element, we explore the process behind shifts toward *tolerance* and *acceptance* – two related but distinct concepts. Verkuyten et al. (2020: 546) describe tolerance as a type of forbearance: "Tolerance shares with discrimination a negative attitude, but prevents this attitude from becoming negative actions." Or as one gay interviewee put it, "tolerating gays for me means that they are not going to punch me in the face because I am gay. That's all."[2] Tolerance is, of course, preferable to discrimination; but it is not an end goal. Van Quaquebeke, Henrich, and Eckloff (2007: 188) draw a useful distinction between tolerance as a reaction to one's "*presence* in the subject's environment," and acceptance as a reaction to one's "*membership* in the subject's group."[3]

The data we present in this Element frequently trace a path that begins with tolerance but later evolves into acceptance and active support. An illustrative example of acceptance, in contrast to tolerance, comes from an interview we conducted with the mother of a gay activist in Argentina. She recounted the experience of sharing that her son was gay with a group of new acquaintances, describing it as her own coming-out experience: "com[ing] out as the mother of

---

[1] By humanization, we refer to a broad set of processes that shift conceptions of outgroup members from stereotypes to complex and individualized depictions, often highlighting universal or shared experiences and emotions.
[2] Author interview, December 2023.
[3] The literature on tolerance provides a variety of different definitions of the concept – some even equating it with acceptance. In the United Nations 1995 Declaration of Principles on Tolerance, the first article ("Meaning of tolerance") opens with: "1.1 Tolerance is respect, acceptance and appreciation of the rich diversity of our world's cultures, our forms of expression and ways of being human." However, we follow more recent scholarship such as van Quaquebeke et al. (2007) and Verkuyten et al. (2020) in acknowledging important differences between tolerance (or toleration) and acceptance.

a gay son." She had reached a place of acceptance wherein her son's sexuality was not simply something she tolerated, but part of her identity as well, as "the mother of a gay son" who concluded that "there was nothing to hide."

The powerful effects of humanization and empathy-building are not limited to close connections. This also arises in repeated positive interactions with strangers. We document shifting attitudes among hospitality workers amid a boom in gay tourism. In this case, behavior led attitudes: Waiters and hotel managers had economic incentives to treat gay clientele with respect – to "act" tolerant – even if they held personal prejudices. But over time, their experiences interacting with customers who were gay changed their attitudes. They began to see them in a more positive light, as respectful customers who paid on time and gave good tips. Eventually, they shifted from "acting" tolerant to genuinely adopting an attitude of tolerance and acceptance.

Scaling up to the aggregate trends of increasing tolerance and acceptance, we also examine macrolevel forces at play that have facilitated these individual-level experiences. Hospitality workers had new incentives to serve gay customers as a result of economic changes: transitions to market capitalism and globalization. As markets globalized, so did mass media – forming another pathway for exposure to positive representations of LGBTQ+ identities even in more rural areas. And demographic shifts – a rise in divorce and nontraditional family and parenting arrangements – fostered more openness to alternative family structures of many kinds, including same-sex relationships.

1.1 The Interplay between Public Opinion and Policy

The primary focus of this Element is on understanding changes in attitudes; but these attitudes are intimately related to public policy. Latin America has experienced an unprecedented expansion of LGBTQ+ rights in recent years. In 2010, Argentina was the first country in the region to legalize same-sex marriage. Since then, seven more countries have followed suit. Today, 79 percent of Latin American citizens live in countries that recognize same-sex marriage.[4] Same-sex adoption, first legalized in Uruguay in 2009, is now legal in six countries, comprising 55 percent of the regional population.[5]

In addition to expanding rights for same-sex couples, some countries in Latin America have been at the forefront of trans rights – particularly Argentina and

---

[4] Among the countries that have not legalized same-sex marriage, Bolivia (home to 2% of Latin America's population) has established civil unions for same-sex partners, and Peru (6% of the region's population) recognizes foreign same-sex marriages.

[5] Most other Latin American countries allow single-parent adoption; the exceptions are El Salvador, Panama, and Paraguay.

Uruguay. Argentina's 2012 Gender Identity Law made it the first country in the world to enable trans people to update their legal documents to reflect their gender identities without barriers such as surgical requirements. And today, nine countries in the region have similar laws. Only thirteen countries around the world legally recognize nonbinary genders; four of them are in Latin America. A recent dataset, the Transgender Rights Indicator Project (TRIP), scores 173 countries around the world on the state of trans rights, considering factors such as legal recognition and antidiscrimination protections (Williamson 2024). On this measure, Uruguay scores higher than any other country in the world.[6]

Recent scholarship has provided insight into how gay and trans Latin Americans won these rights (Corrales 2021) and the potential backlash from conservative and religious forces (Smith & Boas 2023; Zaremberg & Almeida 2022). But to understand the stability of newly won rights – can they withstand political attacks or will future governments roll back LGBTQ+ rights? – we must also understand the landscape of public opinion.

Moreover, societal attitudes influence the implementation of new laws, and negative attitudes can blunt the gains of public policy wins. A law allowing for legal gender changes or same-sex marriage can be undermined if bureaucrats feel empowered to refuse to process these applications. Antidiscrimination laws can only go so far toward actually eliminating discrimination if hostile attitudes abound. And although public opinion shapes what legislation is possible, it is not the case that all policy wins are preceded by groundswells of public support (particularly when new policy is established through the courts as opposed to Congress).[7] Indeed, even in countries that have granted legal rights to LGBTQ+ populations, immense everyday obstacles remain.

Consider Bolivia: based on the legal indicators in the TRIP dataset, it ranks fourteenth in the world for trans rights. Yet, as we will discuss in the next section, only a slight majority of Bolivians approve of trans people having the same rights as other Bolivians and only 40 percent believe their locale is a good place to be gay or lesbian. Brazil was the twelfth country in the world to legalize same-sex marriage; yet it is also home to the highest rate of anti-LGBT hate crimes worldwide (Malta et al. 2019: 12–13).

---

[6] Uruguay scores 12 on a 0–13 scale for each of the last four years of data (2018–2021).

[7] To this point, de Abreu Maia, Chiu, and Desposato (2023) look for evidence that public opinion predicts LGBT policy advances in Latin America and fail to find significant results in their models – highlighting that the relationship between public opinion and policy outcomes is not nearly as clear-cut as democratic theory might suggest. As we discuss in Section 8, activist groups in some countries – such as Bolivia – have been effective in working with lawyers and the courts to advance protections for LGBT citizens even without strong public support.

Legal victories, clearly, do not guarantee widespread acceptance. But the existence of legal protections can enable broader integration into society. And that integration yields further acceptance as more people experience positive interactions with LGBTQ+ individuals.

The strategies that activists pursue to win these public policy battles also contribute to changing public opinion. The most successful activist efforts focused on "winning the streets" – changing public opinion to create pressure for legislative action (Bimbi 2011). A particularly effective approach centered on framing LGBTQ+ rights as *human* rights rather than civil rights. This strategy was effective because it appealed to pre-existing values held by many citizens living in postauthoritarian societies (Encarnación 2016). And it contributed to public opinion change by, again, humanizing groups and building empathy.

1.2 Outline

In this Element, we set out to understand where and why people have moved toward tolerance and acceptance. We bring together quantitative and qualitative data to build a multifaceted account of how attitude change happens, considering individual-level and structural factors. Whereas our quantitative public opinion data provide a broad view of overall trends and comparative levels of tolerance, our qualitative data provide insights into the sources of these attitudes.[8]

In interviews, every person had a unique story of the process by which they came to change their mind. But across our interviews, we identify many commonalities – patterns that are bolstered by public opinion data and historical and archival research. These diverse data sources point to the combined importance of personal interaction with LGBTQ+ people, media representation, economic incentives, demographic changes, and the strategies activists employ to win legal battles for equal rights.

We begin in Section 2 by describing the current landscape of public opinion in the region and showing how attitudes toward LGBTQ+ people have changed over time. There is substantial variation across countries in the level of tolerance toward LGBTQ+ people, but in nearly every country, attitudes have grown more positive over time. One consistent pattern is that younger people hold more positive attitudes toward LGBTQ+ people and rights. The robust relationship between age and tolerance suggests that the overall trend might be driven by generational replacement: Individuals don't necessarily grow more tolerant over time, but each new generation is more accepting than the last.

---

[8] See Online Appendix for details on our qualitative data collection.

But we find evidence that individuals *do* change their minds. Younger cohorts are reliably more tolerant than older cohorts; but over time, every cohort has become more tolerant. And these changes over time within cohorts are often *larger* than the differences across cohorts.

In subsequent sections, we turn to the question of *how* this individual-level attitude change happens, bringing the quantitative public opinion data together with a wealth of new qualitative data.

Section 4 presents qualitative data from interviews with the friends and family of LGBTQ+ individuals. Their stories of reacting to a close friend's or family member's coming out shed light on how people can move from intolerance to acceptance. Among those who previously held negative attitudes toward LGBTQ+ people, none described a sudden change in their attitudes. They did not immediately abandon all prior prejudices when a loved one came out to them. Instead, this revelation marked the beginning of a slow process of grappling with one's assumptions and beliefs. This process did not always end with complete acceptance – or even basic tolerance. But for many, it led them to gradually change both attitudes and behavior in fundamental ways.

Section 5 explores how interpersonal contact can foster tolerance and acceptance in a very different context, looking at the experiences of hospitality workers encountering LGBTQ+ customers. Whereas Section 4 focused on relationships among close friends and family members, here we consider interactions among strangers. Drawing on interviews with waiters, hotel managers, and other workers in the hospitality industry, we trace a very different trajectory toward tolerance and acceptance. Here, we see people changing their *behavior* first, their *attitudes* later. Amid a transition to market capitalism and a boom in international tourism, hospitality workers had new economic incentives to serve gay and lesbian customers. Many of these workers held strong prejudices against LGBTQ+ communities, but they saw an economic interest in "acting as if"[9] they did not mind their customers' sexual orientations. Over time, however, they had repeated positive interactions with gay and lesbian customers. And these interactions changed their perceptions of these groups. As a result of treating gay and lesbian customers with respect for economic reasons, they began to more sincerely tolerate – or even accept – those with different sexual orientations.

Direct interactions are not the only source of attitude change. Recent decades have also brought a sea change in how LGBTQ+ narratives appear in popular culture. From the appearance of gay and lesbian characters on television shows to the transformation of pride from small countercultural marches to massive

---

[9] A concept borrowed from Wedeen (2009).

parades with corporate sponsors, LGBTQ+ communities are more visible than ever. In Section 6, we discuss the positive effects of representation in the media, as well as the drawbacks to the respectability politics that have come along with mainstream media representation.

Section 7 turns to the role of broad demographic changes. The late twentieth century was a time of change for Latin American family structures, with divorce legalization and the rise of blended families. Exposure to different kinds of families and parenting arrangements influenced attitudes about traditional family structures, opening the door for activists to fight for same-sex marriage and adoption rights and helping many parents of LGBTQ+ children to let go of long-held expectations and embrace the families their children would go on to build for themselves.

Finally, in Section 8, we discuss the relationship between LGBTQ+ rights and acceptance. In some cases, savvy activists have managed to win new rights for LGBTQ+ communities even when public opinion was against them. Formally establishing legal rights is a crucial step on the path toward broader societal acceptance. But when these laws lack public support, their impact is blunted and they are vulnerable to being reversed in a future administration or undermined by poor implementation. When activist groups prioritize changing hearts and minds (alongside legal strategies and appeals to politicians), their legal victories go much further in moving society toward equality and acceptance. Where activists were most successful in changing hearts and minds, two key strategic decisions underlie their success: maintaining some distance from political parties (to avoid locking an issue into perpetual partisan divisions), and framing LGBTQ+ rights as human rights (appealing to preexisting values in postauthoritarian societies).

We conclude with a discussion of what lies ahead. Can we expect the progress toward tolerance and acceptance to continue? Is there a risk of public opinion backlash or the loss of hard-won rights? How might the path for trans rights emulate or diverge from the path for rights of LGB individuals?

2 The Current Landscape of Public Opinion

Attitudes toward LGBTQ+ people vary widely across Latin America. As of March 2025, thirty-eight countries around the world have legalized same-sex marriage.[10] One quarter of those countries are in Latin America.[11] South America, in particular, has some of the most widespread legal protections

---

[10] See www.hrc.org/resources/marriage-equality-around-the-world, accessed April 16, 2025.
[11] Argentina, Brazil, Chile, Colombia, Costa Rica, Cuba, Ecuador, Mexico, and Uruguay.

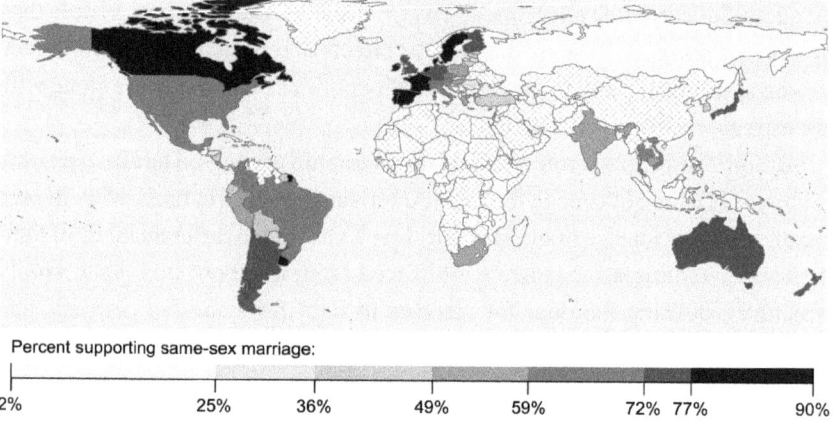

Figure 1 Support for same-sex marriage around the world.
Note: Data come from from AmericasBarometer (2023), Eurobarometer (2023), Pew Global Attitudes (2023), and Ipsos (2021 and 2023). All survey projects had overlapping geographic coverage, enabling adjustments for differences in question wording and other survey-project effects. Missing countries are marked with cross-hatching. See Online Appendix for details on how we made these adjustments.

for LGBTQ+ individuals. Comparing Africa, Asia, Europe, North America, Oceania, and South America – South America ranks first in the proportion of countries where same-sex marriage is legal (50 percent),[12] citizens have the right to change their legal gender (58 percent),[13] nonbinary genders are recognized (25 percent),[14] and conversion therapy is banned (67 percent).[15] But even within those countries that have stood at the forefront of LGBTQ+ rights expansion, public support is not universal. And in much of Central America, where LGBTQ+ people have not seen the same legal victories as many in South America, attitudes toward same-sex marriage and other rights remain negative.

Figure 1 provides a broad view of support for same-sex marriage around the world. The data presented in Figure 1 are drawn from 141 surveys conducted between 2021 and 2023, covering seventy-five countries.[16] The survey-adjusted approval estimates illustrated in Figure 1 range from 90 percent approval in Denmark, to 2% approval in Nigeria. Countries are grouped into septiles, with black indicating the highest approval (77–90 percent) and light gray the lowest approval (2–25 percent).

---

[12] www.equaldex.com/issue/marriage, accessed April 16, 2025.
[13] www.equaldex.com/issue/changing-gender, accessed April 16, 2025.
[14] www.equaldex.com/issue/non-binary-gender-recognition, accessed April 16, 2025.
[15] www.equaldex.com/issue/conversion-therapy, accessed April 16, 2025.
[16] See Online Appendix for details on how the relative measure presented here was constructed to harmonize across different survey projects and question wordings.

Uruguay ranks fourth among all 75 countries included in the analysis, with an estimated approval rate of 83 percent.[17] At 74 percent, Chile and Argentina also rank among the most supportive. Support for same-sex marriage in Mexico is slightly higher than in the United States (69 percent versus 64 percent). Support is lower in the Andean countries, with moderate levels of support in Peru (54 percent) and Colombia (60 percent), and fairly low support in Ecuador (41 percent) and Bolivia (40 percent). Support falls much lower in Central America, with only 25 percent support in Guatemala and Honduras, and 22 percent in Panama. Though even here, attitudes toward same-sex marriage do not come close to the overwhelming opposition seen in parts of Africa, Asia, and Eastern Europe (only 2 percent of Nigerians, 5 percent of Indonesians, and 14 percent of Bulgarians support same-sex marriage).

Zooming in on the Americas, Figure 2 breaks down the strength of support and opposition to same-sex marriage in 23 countries in Latin America and the Caribbean, plus the United States and Canada. Figure 2 presents data from the Latin American Public Opinion Project's (LAPOP's) 2023 AmericasBarometer surveys. (Note that the approval ratings in Figure 2 differ from those in the cross-regional map because the map incorporated adjustments for comparability across survey projects; here, we present the raw values from the AmericasBarometer surveys.) As illustrated in Figure 2, a majority of citizens support same-sex marriage in the northernmost countries of North America – Canada (76 percent), the United States (56 percent), and Mexico (62 percent) – and in the southernmost countries of South America – Chile (67 percent), Argentina (72 percent), Uruguay (79 percent), and Brazil (56 percent).

Paraguay is nearly a mirror image of its neighbors in the Southern Cone, with 76 percent *disapproving* of same-sex marriage. Across the Andean region and Central America, support ranges from around 45 percent (Costa Rica, Colombia, Nicaragua) to about 20 percent (Honduras, Guatemala, Panama). The strongest opposition lies in the Caribbean: only 13 percent of Bahamians and 16 percent of Grenadians and Jamaicans support same-sex marriage.

As is evident from Figure 2, same-sex marriage is a highly polarizing issue. On a ten-point approval scale, most citizens indicate either the strongest possible approval (10) or the strongest possible disapproval (1). Across all 25 countries, an average of 61 percent of respondents placed themselves at either of the two extremes. In only four countries did fewer than 50 percent select one

---

[17] These estimated approval ratings are the percent of respondents who approve of same-sex marriage, excluding those who did not respond. So, for example, in a survey of 100 individuals, if 45 said they support same-sex marriage, 45 opposed it, and another 10 did not answer, the estimated approval rating would be 50 percent. See Online Appendix for further details.

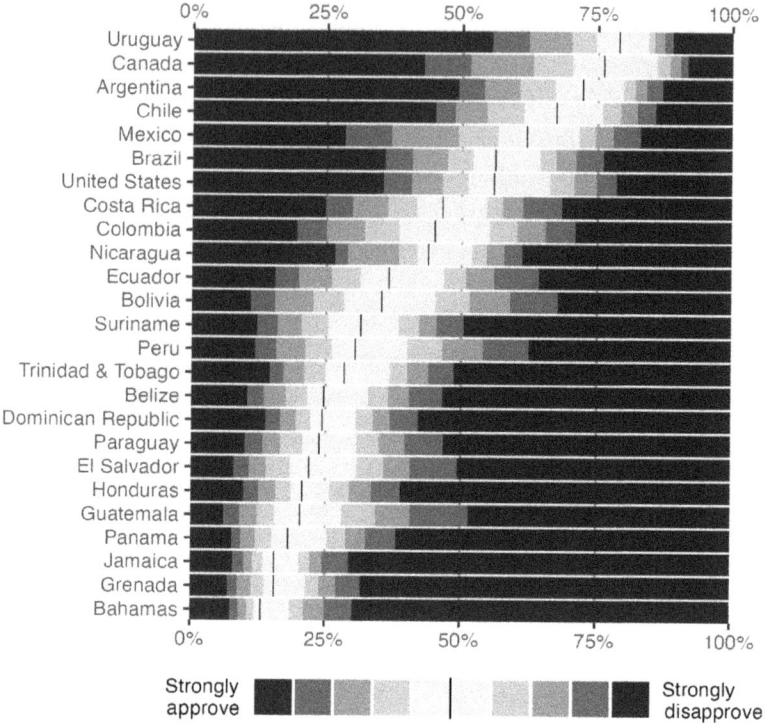

Figure 2 Support for same-sex marriage in the Americas.
Note: AmericasBarometer 2023.

of these two extremes: Bolivia (43 percent), Mexico (46 percent), Colombia (49 percent), and Peru (49 percent). Even in these four least-polarized contexts, more than four in ten respondents selected the most extreme response options; and only 14–17 percent placed themselves in the middle of the scale (at a five or six).[18] Jamaicans were the most likely to select an extreme response: 71 percent indicated the strongest possible disapproval and 8 percent the strongest possible approval. In Uruguay, the most pro-same-sex-marriage country, two-thirds of respondents selected one of the two extremes, with 56 percent indicating the strongest possible approval and 11 percent the strongest possible disapproval. Canadians, who are almost as likely as Uruguayans to approve of same-sex marriage, do not express their positions as strongly: only 43 percent indicate the strongest approval and 8 percent the strongest disapproval.

Looking beyond the single issue of same-sex marriage, Figure 3 presents data from a 2023 Gallup survey that asked citizens in 123 countries whether

---

[18] Across all countries, an average of 12 percent placed themselves in the middle of the scale, ranging from 6 percent in the Bahamas to 17 percent in Bolivia.

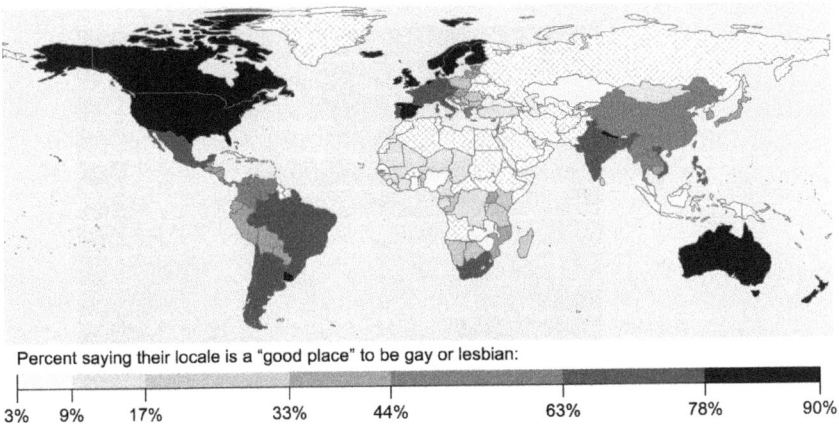

Figure 3 Percent describing their locale as a "good place" for gay and lesbian people to live.

Note: Gallup 2023 data. Missing countries are marked with cross-hatching.

the place they currently reside is a "good place" for gay and lesbian people to live. Seventy-nine percent of Uruguayans answered in the affirmative, making Uruguay the sixteenth best place (by citizen perception) to be gay or lesbian. Brazil ranked twenty-fourth, Mexico twenty-seventh, Chile twenty-eighth, and Argentina thirtieth. On the other end of the spectrum, Paraguayan citizens deemed their country the least hospitable in Latin America, with only 34 percent describing it as a good place for gay and lesbian people to live (putting it in the bottom half of countries surveyed – sixty-eighth out of 123). In Central America, Costa Rica was the only country in which a majority (62 percent) said that it was a good place to be gay or lesbian.

2.1 Trans Rights

The data presented thus far have focused on issues specific to lesbian, gay, and bisexual people. What about attitudes toward transgender and nonbinary people? Comparatively little data is available on attitudes toward trans people and on trans-specific policy issues. But recent data collected by the Latin American Public Opinion Project suggests that Latin Americans do not hold dramatically different attitudes about basic rights for trans people versus lesbian, gay, and bisexual (LGB) people. Support for trans rights is lower, but not dramatically so; and people have stronger opinions on LGB rights than on trans rights.[19]

---

[19] See also Castorena et al. (2024).

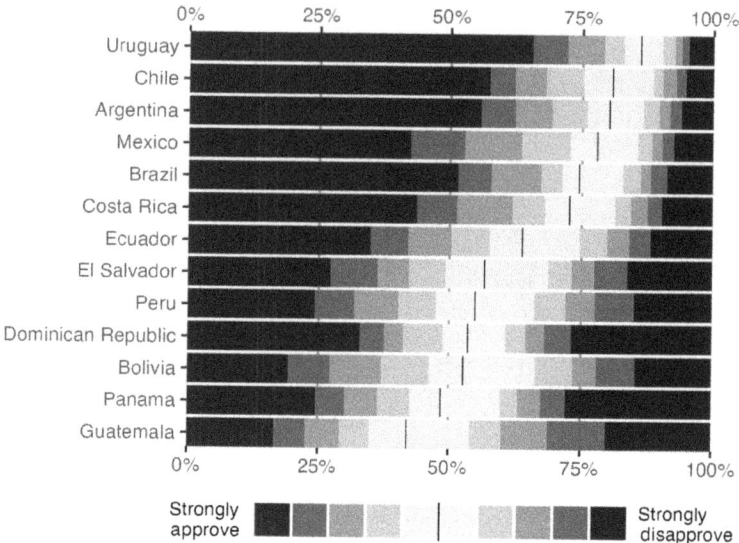

Figure 4 Support for equal rights (LGB).
Note: "How strongly do you approve or disapprove of people from sexual minorities, such as gay, lesbian, bisexual, etc., having the same rights as the majority of (nationality)?"
Source: 2023 AmericasBarometer.

The 2023 wave of the AmericasBarometer surveys asked respondents whether they approved of LGBT individuals having equal rights – but the question was asked separately for LGB individuals ("sexual minorities") and trans and nonbinary individuals ("gender minorities"). Using a split-sample design, respondents were randomly assigned to see one of the following questions:

> "How strongly do you approve or disapprove of people from sexual minorities, such as gay, lesbian, bisexual, etc., having the same rights as the majority of (nationality)?"

> "How strongly do you approve or disapprove of people from gender minorities, such as nonbinary, transgender, etc., having the same rights as the majority of (nationality)?"

The responses to these questions in 13 Latin American countries are illustrated in Figures 4 and 5. We do not observe dramatically different levels of acceptance for LGB people versus transgender and nonbinary people in these data. Overall, 65 percent express at least weak support for equal rights for LGB people and 63 percent for trans people.[20] The largest within-country differences

---

[20] "At least weak support" is defined as a response of six or higher on the 1–10 scale.

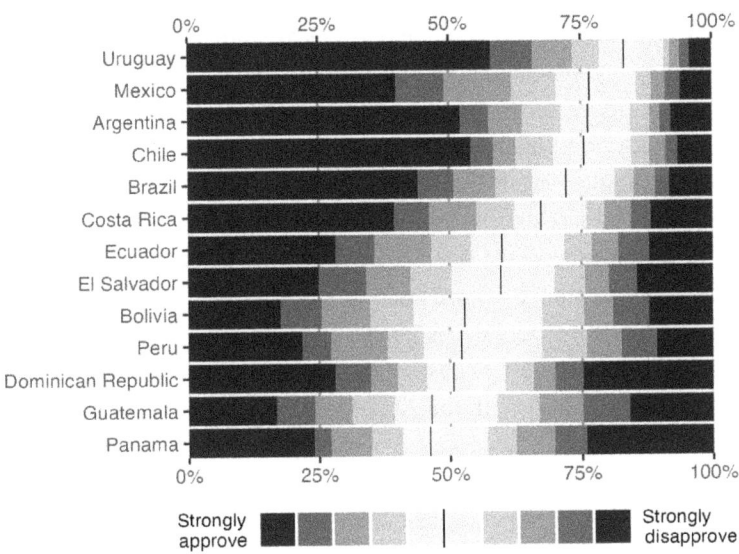

Figure 5 Support for Equal Rights (Trans).
Note: LAPOP 2023 data. "How strongly do you approve or disapprove of people from gender minorities, such as non-binary, transgender, etc., having the same rights as the majority of (nationality)?"

occur in Costa Rica and Chile, where respondents are 5 percentage points more likely to support equal rights for sexual minorities than for gender minorities.

The greater support for sexual-minority rights is statistically significant ($p < 0.01$), but substantively small: when asked about gender minorities, respondents move down about 0.14 points on a ten-point scale.[21]

Across all countries, respondents tend to have stronger opinions on LGB rights than on trans rights (significant at $p < 0.001$).[22] On average, they are five percentage points more likely to express maximum approval (10) or disapproval (1) when asked about LGB rights. The difference in strength of opinion is especially stark in Uruguay and Brazil (where respondents are eight percentage points more likely to place themselves at one of the two extremes on

---

[21] This estimate comes from two linear regressions. The first is a bivariate model, regressing support on the reference group (LGB vs T); the second adds country fixed effects. In both cases, the coefficient estimate and significance level remain the same. See Online Appendix for full regression details.

[22] Significance estimate comes from two linear regressions (one with and one without country fixed effects). We create a folded scale, where responses of one and ten are coded as "5" on the extremity scale, two and nine are coded as "4", etc. We then regress these folded responses on the question type. Both with and without country fixed effects, the estimated coefficient on the gender minorities question (with the sexual minorities question as the reference group) is −0.15 with a standard error of 0.02.

support for LGB rights), and quite modest in Argentina, Chile, and Costa Rica (with only a two percentage-point difference).

These data suggest that overall attitudes toward trans people and LGB people are only marginally different, with slightly more support for LGB people and slightly stronger opinions (both positive and negative) about LGB people. But these data should be interpreted with caution. The question – should these groups have the same rights as everyone else? – gives insight into a basic level of tolerance toward each group. But the differences in attitudes might be starker if we were to ask people about specific rights.

Take the United States, for example, where survey firms have polled on specific trans rights issues. In the AmericasBarometer US survey, 74 percent expressed at least weak support for equal rights for LGB people versus 67 percent for trans and nonbinary people. But turning to specific rights relevant to each group, the gap widens. The 2020 American National Election Study (ANES) asked respondents for their attitudes on same-sex marriage and on bathroom access for transgender individuals. Sixty-seven percent supported same-sex marriage (and another 18 percent supported civil unions); only 51 percent said that transgender people should be able to use the bathroom that aligns with their gender. When LAPOP asked about general support for equal rights, we saw a gap of seven percentage points in attitudes toward LGB versus trans rights; but when the ANES asked about two specific rights, that gap more than doubled, to 16 percentage points.

We see some evidence of this dynamic in Chile. Recall that the LAPOP surveys found only a two-percentage-point gap in Chileans' approval of equal rights for LGB versus trans people, when framed in the abstract. But recent surveys from Cadem, a major polling firm in Chile, asked about specific rights for both LGB and trans people. And we observe a consistent and sizable difference in approval for LGB versus trans rights. We consider two pairs of questions – distinguished by whether the issues at hand involve children (adoption; gender change for minors) or not (same-sex marriage; gender change for adults). In the August 2023 survey, approval for same-sex marriage (72 percent) was ten percentage points higher than approval of a trans adult's right to legally change their gender (62 percent). On issues involving children, the LGB-trans gap is even larger: 59 percent approve of same-sex adoption, whereas only 44 percent approve of the right for minors to legally change their gender with parental approval.

Scholars have long observed that people tend to express greater support for general liberties than for specific rights (Prothro & Grigg 1960).[23] There are a

---

[23] See also Jones et al. (2018).

variety of potential reasons for this gap in support for abstract versus concrete rights, and people can hold these seemingly discordant views without much cognitive dissonance. One way that people might reconcile these views is by redefining "equal" rights versus "special" rights. A supporter of same-sex marriage might argue that equality means that everyone should have the right to marry whomever they love; an opponent might argue that having the "same rights" as everyone else simply means that, for example, a gay man, like a heterosexual man, has the right to marry a woman. Similarly, one could argue that every individual has a right to legal documents that accurately reflect their gender – so transgender individuals should be able to change their legal identification and birth certificates to match their gender, even if it conflicts with the sex assigned at birth. But someone opposed to legally recognizing transgender identities might argue that as long as no one is allowed to change their legal gender, the system is equal; and allowing legal gender changes for transgender individuals would constitute granting a "special" right. Hence some respondents state – sincerely – that they support the idea of LGBT people having equal rights; but when asked about specific rights relevant to these groups, they express opposition. Each measure is informative: support for general rights can tell us something about broader attitudes toward a group; whereas support for specific, concrete rights is likely to be more informative for political behavior.

2.2 Demographic Predictors

Figures 4 and 5 showed that citizens within a given country hold diverse opinions about LGBTQ+ rights and individuals. What explains the variation within countries? That is, what characteristics are associated with higher or lower levels of tolerance and acceptance?

Prior research has found that the demographic predictors of support for LGBTQ+ rights in Latin America are a familiar set of variables that predict support in other regions. Support for same-sex marriage is higher among urban-dwellers; wealthier and more educated individuals; women; young people; and those who are not religious or for whom religion is not very important (Lodola & Corral 2010).[24] The predictors are similar for support for transgender rights and for general attitudes toward LGBT individuals.[25]

---

[24] See also Dion and Díez (2017, 2022); Díez and Dion (2018); González-Rostani and Morgenstern (2023).

[25] See, among others, Adamczyk and Pitt (2009); Chaux et al. (2021); Jung and Tavits (2024); Paradela-López, Antón, and Jima-González (2023); Seligson, Morales, and Russo (2019) on attitudes toward LGB individuals. See Flores (2015); Norton and Herek (2013) on trans rights.

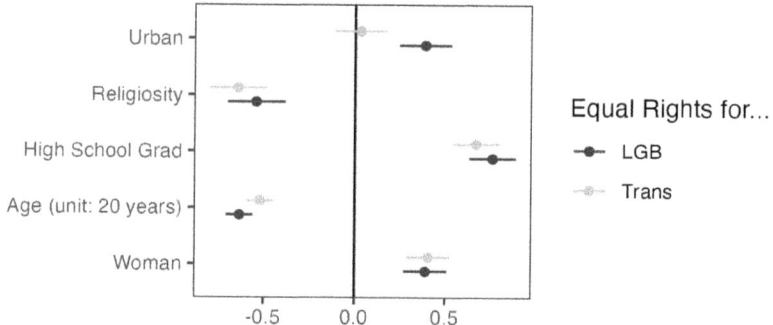

Figure 6 Predicting support for equal rights.
Note: Black points mark the estimated coefficients from a regression of the sexual minorities equal rights question on gender (see fn. 26), urban/rural residence, religiosity (a binary variable indicating whether religion is "somewhat" or "very" important), education (binary variable indicating whether one completed high school), and age (divided by 20, for easier comparison with dummy variables). The model also included country fixed effects. Grey points indicate the same for the gender minorities question. Error bars indicate 95 percent confidence intervals.

The most recent AmericasBarometer surveys show similar patterns. Figure 6 illustrates the results from two regressions: one predicting support for LGB rights and the other for trans rights. Urban residence, education, gender, age, and religiosity are all statistically significant predictors of support for equal rights for LGB individuals (with higher support among those who are younger, less religious, more educated, living in urban areas, and women).[26] The same is true of support for equal rights for trans and nonbinary individuals, with one exception: urban residence is not significant. Indeed, even in the case of equal rights for LGB individuals, where urban residence is a significant predictor, it is less predictive than any of the other demographic variables we include.[27]

Figure 7 breaks the analysis down by country. We can see that age is the most consistent predictor across countries ($p < 0.05$ in 24 of the 26 models). High school education is also a reliable predictor (significant in 20 of 26 models). Religiosity, gender, and urban residence are less reliable predictors across the region.

---

[26] Estimates come from an OLS model including country fixed effects, with a $p < 0.05$ threshold for significance. We measure education with a dummy variable for complete high school education or higher, and religiosity with a dummy variable for whether they state that religion is "somewhat" or "very" important. For gender, we include three control variables: woman, nonbinary, and missing (in the 2023 round of AmericasBarometer, respondents were asked to self-identify their gender, but some did not respond; 1.3 percent of respondents in the countries we analyze were missing gender data and 0.1 percent identified as nonbinary). See Online Appendix for full regression details.

[27] When we remove the urban residence variable from the model, the adjusted R^2 is virtually unchanged (it drops by 0.002). See Online Appendix.

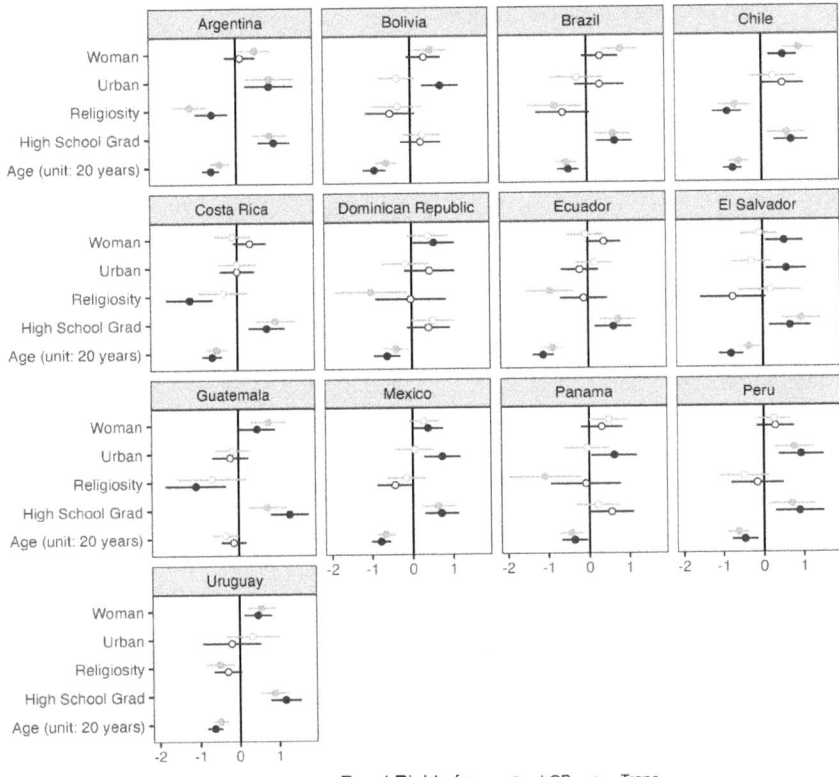

Figure 7 Predicting support for equal rights by country.
Note: Black points indicate the estimated coefficients from a regression of the sexual minorities rights question on gender, urban/rural residence, religiosity (a binary variable indicating whether religion is "somewhat" or "very" important), education (binary variable indicating whether one completed high school), and age (divided by 20, for easier comparison with dummy variables). Grey points indicate the same for the gender minorities question. Error bars indicate 95 percent confidence intervals. Solid points indicate that the estimate is significant at $p < 0.05$; hollow points indicate the coefficient does not reach $p < 0.05$ significance.

2.3 Shifting Attitudes over Time

The preceding sections presented a snapshot in time, reporting attitudes toward LGBTQ+ people in the current moment. But how did we get here? Have attitudes mostly held steady over the years? Grown consistently more positive in recent decades? Bounced up and down over time, with surges of both support and backlash?

Time-series data on attitudes toward LGBTQ+ people is limited; many surveys did not begin asking these questions until fairly recently. But the World Values Survey (WVS) has asked one question relevant for gauging basic

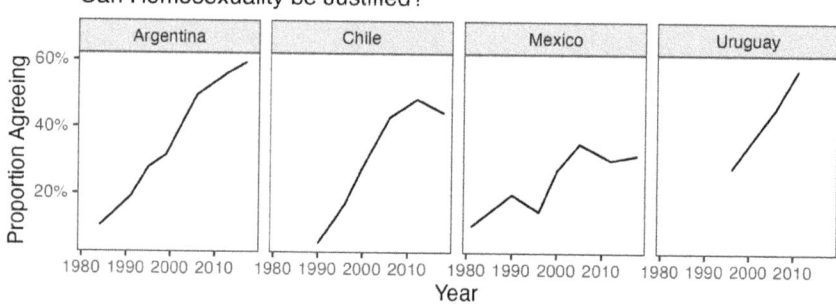

Figure 8 Tolerance in the Southern Cone and Mexico, 1981–2018.
Note: World Values Survey data.

tolerance since the 1980s in Argentina and Mexico, and since the 1990s in Chile and Uruguay. The WVS asks respondents:

"Can homosexuality be justified?"

In these four countries, attitudes have shifted quite steadily in a more positive direction over the past few decades. (Notably, these are the four countries with the highest levels of popular support for LGBT rights in Latin America today – see Figures 4 and 5.) Figure 8 illustrates long-term trends in attitudes toward gay people in Argentina, Chile, Mexico and Uruguay. From 1980–1990, about 5–20 percent of respondents agreed that "homosexuality can be justified." By the 2010s, attitudes had shifted dramatically. Agreement in Mexico nearly tripled from 11 percent to 32 percent. In Chile, it jumped from 5 percent to 44 percent. And in Argentina and Uruguay, it reached 58–59 percent in the most recent surveys.

These positive trends are not limited to the most accepting countries of the Southern Cone and Mexico. LAPOP's AmericasBarometer surveys have asked questions about LGB rights across Latin America and the Caribbean for two decades. Figure 9 shows trends in attitudes on two questions:

- Thinking of homosexuals, how strongly do you approve or disapprove of such people being permitted to run for public office?
- How strongly do you approve or disapprove of same-sex couples having the right to marry?

Respondents were asked to indicate their approval/disapproval on a ten-point scale (1 = strongly disapprove; 10 = strongly approve).

We see, once again, wide variation in attitudes across countries. But nearly every country shows at least some movement toward tolerance over time. Regressing support for same-sex marriage on the survey year, Panama is the

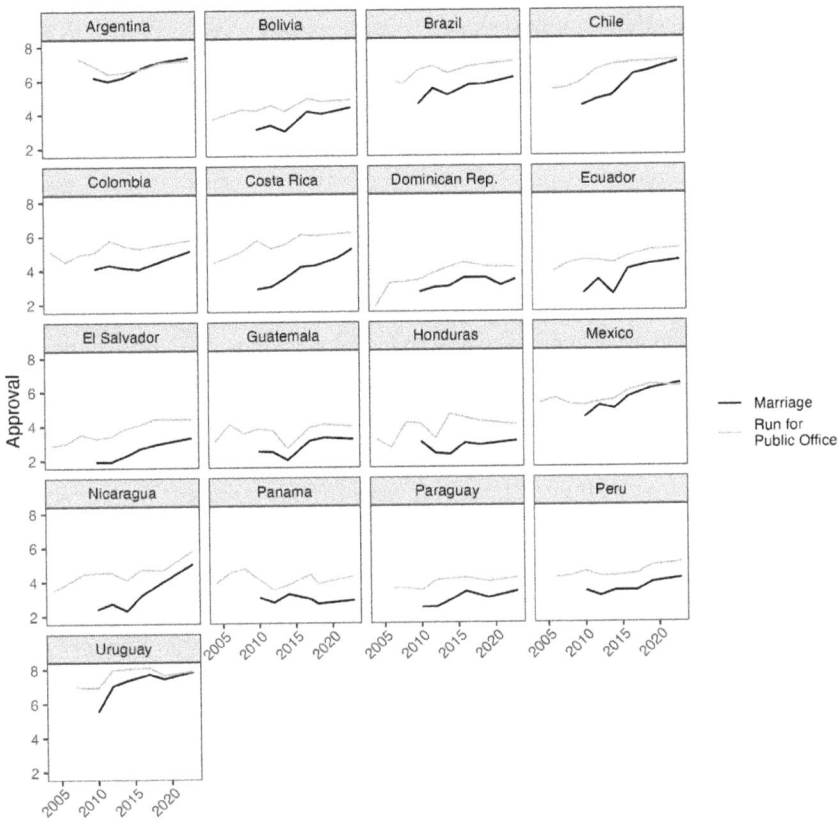

Figure 9 Tolerance in Latin America, 2002–2023.
Note: AmericasBarometer 2023 data on support for same-sex marriage and the right of homosexuals to run for office. "Approval" is calculated as the average score on a 1–10 scale (where 10 indicates maximum approval, 1 maximum disapproval).

only country in which we do not find a statistically significant positive trend (using a threshold of $p < 0.05$). In Panama, we see a slight downward trend ($p < 0.05$), with an estimated trend of −0.019 per year on the ten-point approval scale. Note, however, that the magnitude of this negative trend is smaller than that of the positive trends observed in all other countries. The smallest estimated positive trend is in Honduras, where each year is associated with a 0.024-point increase in approval. And the steepest trends – observed in Chile and Nicaragua – are approximately ten times as large (0.21 per year).[28]

On the right to run for public office, we observe a statistically significant positive trend in 15 of 17 countries. The only exceptions are Panama, where we again see a slightly negative (−0.006) estimated annual trend (but this time

---

[28] See Online Appendix for full regression results across countries.

it is not statistically significant), and Argentina, with a very small (0.01) and insignificant estimated annual increase.

Across the region, we see a steady – if mostly slow – shift toward greater tolerance and support for LGBT rights.

2.4 Generational Replacement versus Changing Minds

What lies behind the shift toward greater tolerance and acceptance of LGBTQ+ communities? A common explanation for this pattern is that younger generations are more accepting of gay and lesbian people. Amid the "continual replacement of older, more prejudiced cohorts with younger, less prejudiced ones [...] societies on the whole can become more tolerant, even though no single individual does" (Firebaugh & Davis 1988: 253).

As we saw in Section 2.2, age is one of the strongest predictors of attitudes on LGBTQ+ rights. Younger generations consistently hold more positive attitudes toward LGBTQ+ individuals and rights. Figure 10 presents the same World Values Survey data from Figure 8, this time broken down by generational cohorts. Lighter lines indicate younger cohorts. Younger people are almost always more accepting than older people (lighter lines almost always remain above darker lines). But the trend toward more acceptance

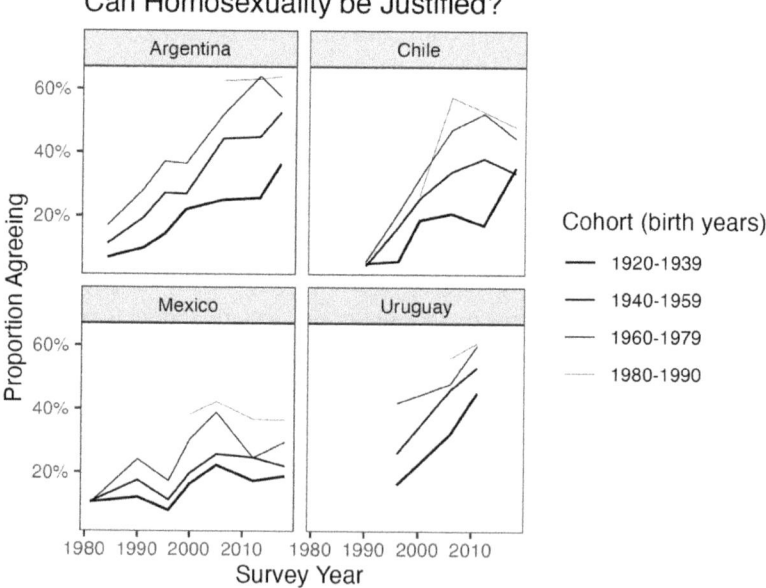

Figure 10 Tolerance by generation.
Note: World Values Survey data.

is not just a byproduct of generational replacement. We also observe dramatic shifts within cohorts.

Consider Argentina. In the most recent data, from 2017, 64 percent of citizens born between 1980 and 1990 agree that "homosexuality can be justified" – a rate of agreement 28 percentage points higher than that of those born from 1920 to 1939. But comparing attitudes over time within cohorts, we see an even larger shift from 1984 to 2017. Agreement increased by 29 percentage points in the 1920–1939 cohort, and by 42 percentage points in the 1940–1959 cohort.

The story looks similar in Uruguay and in Chile. In Mexico, the trend toward tolerance has been slower – reflected in the lower levels of tolerance among the even the youngest generation, and in smaller shifts over time among older people. But the pattern of increasing tolerance within generations is still seen in Mexico, even if it is less stark.

Public opinion data show that attitudes toward LGBTQ+ people have become much more positive over time in Latin America. Substantial diversity exists in these attitudes: countries in the Southern Cone and Mexico have trended more quickly toward acceptance than many others in the region, and attitudes vary within country by age, education, religiosity, and other demographic factors. But as a whole, the long-term trends evince a positive shift.

One key takeaway from the public opinion data is that change happens at the individual level. The shift toward acceptance is not simply one of generational replacement – where younger generations are more accepting than older ones, and over time the natural generational replacement yields a more accepting population. To the contrary, changes in attitudes over time *within* generations are often as large – or larger than – the differences across generations.

In the following sections, we delve into the question of how and when individual-level attitude change occurs. To explain the mechanisms behind individual-level opinion change, we turn to qualitative data from extensive interviews in selected countries, secondary sources, and archival data.

3 How Does Attitude Change Happen?

Prior literature on reducing prejudice and building tolerance points to the importance of direct contact between individuals from different groups, and of building empathy for members of outgroups. One of the most influential developments in this literature is that of *contact theory*. Contact theory posits that interpersonal contact is one of the most effective means to reduce prejudice between majority and minority group members (Allport 1954; Brown & Hewstone 2005; Pettigrew 1998). The idea is simple but powerful:

getting to know people from other groups – whether defined by ethnicity, race, nationality, sexuality, or any other group identity – can reduce feelings of threat and anxiety and facilitate empathy and understanding. It is harder to paint members of an out-group as threatening, malicious, or evil once people have gotten to know some of those out-group members and begin to see them as complex individuals who differ from them in some ways, yet also share some of their own experiences, ideas, or basic values.

The contact hypothesis lays out a few key conditions that facilitate intergroup prejudice reduction: cooperation toward common goals, participants seeing themselves as holding roughly equal status, and contact being sustained over time and "nonsuperficial" (Allport 1954; Schiappa, Gregg, & Hewes 2006). Some research has found that contact theory can still reduce prejudice in the absence of these ideal conditions (Pettigrew & Tropp 2006: 766). But recent work looking at prejudice across partisan groups found that the equal-status condition was essential to long-term attitude change (Greene et al. 2024). The importance of the ideal conditions likely differs according to the types of out-groups considered.

Looking specifically at attitudes toward LGB individuals, previous studies have found mixed evidence for the contact hypothesis. Observational studies have found that people who have gay friends or relatives hold more positive attitudes toward gay people (Herek & Capitanio 1996; Herek & Glunt 1993). But it is not clear from these studies whether contact drives attitudes; after all, those who already hold positive attitudes are more likely to develop close relationships with gay people. And even when looking at change in attitudes over time, new relationships might be predicted by one's open-mindedness and propensity to change their views.

More recent studies of LGB acceptance have found evidence to support the contact hypothesis – that contact is *driving* some of these positive attitudes (Lewis 2011). But the effects appear to be conditional, with contact having no apparent effect on some individuals, such as white Protestants in the United States (Bramlett 2012; see also Skipworth et al. 2010). And some studies have found that contact can even have a negative effect among certain subgroups. Dyck and Pearson-Merkowitz (2012) find evidence for an intergroup conflict or threat hypothesis among evangelical Christians in the United States: proximity to larger gay populations increased opposition to same-sex marriage among this group.

In a series of recent experiments, Broockman and Kalla find compelling evidence that interpersonal conversations can reduce prejudice toward trans people, with effects that persist over time. Broockman and Kalla (2016) sent canvassers – some trans, others not – to knock on people's doors, inform them that they might face an upcoming voting decision about a law on trans rights, and engage them in a conversation about the issue. The canvassers implemented a strategy encouraging "analogic perspective-taking": exchanging personal narratives of times they "were judged negatively for being different" (221) and encouraging participants to consider how their own experiences relate to trans people's experiences. They found that a single conversation of approximately 10 minutes significantly reduced anti-trans prejudice, with effects lasting at least three months. Notably, the intervention worked regardless of whether the canvasser was trans.

In further experiments, Kalla and Broockman (2020) show that these perspective-taking interventions work even when they are not conducted in person: canvassers sharing narratives over the phone or from a third party in a video message still reduced anti-trans prejudice. A related experiment the authors conducted with regard to attitudes toward unauthorized immigrants highlights the key role of perspective-getting conversations: conversations deploying arguments alone did nothing to reduce prejudice; it was only when these arguments were supplemented by a perspective-getting exercise that they saw a reduction in prejudice.

These studies point to the importance of fostering empathy and understanding across groups. One common way of fostering empathy is through direct contact with an outgroup member (as theorized in the contact hypothesis); Broockman and Kalla identify another mechanism for building empathy, via perspective-taking, which may or may not involve direct contact with an outgroup member.

The studies discussed earlier draw on data from large surveys or experiments. The large surveys provide a broad view of who is more or less accepting; the experiments allow researchers to manipulate conditions to gain causal leverage to better understand the mechanisms underlying the correlations we observe in prior survey research. But these research strategies also face limitations, particularly when it comes to slower, long-term processes. In the following sections, we present a wealth of original qualitative data that complements and builds on existing survey-based and experimental research. Our qualitative data add richness to our understanding of how change happens; point to the importance of slow, gradual processes of attitude change; and illustrate that even contact that does not fit the traditional scope of contact theory (equal status, sustained interaction, cooperation toward common goals) has played a central role in increasing tolerance toward and acceptance of LGBTQ+ individuals.

Our qualitative data come from 66 interviews we conducted from 2023 through 2025. The populations interviewed included LGBTQ+ individuals; friends and family of LGBTQ+ individuals; hospitality workers; and activists.

Interviews ranged in duration from 20 minutes to three hours. Interviewees came from Argentina, Brazil, Chile, Colombia, the Dominican Republic, Honduras, Jamaica, Mexico, Peru, and Puerto Rico. The LGBTQ+ individuals we interviewed ranged in age from 20 to 50, some having come out in just the last five years, while others came out in the 1980s. Among those who were not LGBTQ+ themselves but had an LGBTQ+ friend or family member, ages ranged from 25 to 79. They included 13 parents, five siblings, and five friends. The majority of our interviewees spoke about experiences of being lesbian, gay, or bisexual, or of knowing someone who was lesbian, gay, or bisexual. Eight of our interviewees were either trans or related to someone trans. Our interviews with hospitality workers included 11 waitstaff and bartenders and seven hotel staff, all working in Buenos Aires.

In line with prior research, these interviews again highlight the importance of fostering empathy and understanding to build tolerance and acceptance. But they also illustrate that attitude change often occurs very slowly – in many cases taking months or years to materialize. Some of this long-term attitude change occurs through channels that fall well outside the scope of traditional contact theory. For example, waiters working amid a gay tourism boom had economic incentives to treat gay customers with respect, despite holding negative attitudes toward these customers (hardly an "equal status" interaction). But over time, they gradually became more tolerant and accepting as a result of those interactions. These gradual, long-term dynamics help to explain the magnitude of attitudinal change in recent decades across many Latin American countries.

4 When Friends and Family Come Out

A unique characteristic that distinguishes the dynamics of LGBTQ+ acceptance from other forms of inter-group prejudice reduction is that people often *know* an LGBTQ+ person long before they *learn* that they know an LGBTQ+ person. Thinking about other salient group identities, people tend to know early on whether someone is a member of a different racial or ethnic group, nationality, economic class, or religion. Of course, there are exceptions; but most often, where these are salient group identities, they are also pieces of information that people learn early on in their relationship with someone. But sexual orientation and transgender identity are often revealed later. Family members, in particular, develop close relationships with their LGBTQ+ children or siblings long before learning that they are LGBTQ+.

For those who hold anti-LGBTQ+ attitudes, the revelation that a loved one is LGBTQ+ creates a strong tension in their beliefs. Suddenly, they are forced to reconcile two strongly held attitudes that are now in conflict. If you despise gay people and you love your son, but now you learn that your son is gay – do you stop loving your son or stop despising gay people?[29]

People can resolve this tension by changing their beliefs about LGBTQ+ people, becoming more tolerant and accepting. Or, people can take the opposite approach to resolving the tension in their beliefs: they hold fast to their anti-LGBTQ+ attitudes and reject their friend or relative upon learning that they are LGBTQ+. In practice, the way that people deal with these tensions is often messier. We heard from interviewees who do not attend same-sex-wedding ceremonies, but are present at the receptions; or choose not to attend either event, but welcome the couples to their homes for dinners.

In this section, we draw from interviews we conducted with LGBTQ+ people from around Latin America and, crucially, their friends and family. These interviews illuminate how the coming out of sons, daughters, siblings, and close friends affects the attitudes of parents, siblings, and close friends. Many of our gay and lesbian interviewees remarked that they have told their coming out story so many times that in some cases they even have shorter or longer versions ready to go for different audiences. But parents, siblings, and friends have their own stories of understanding that are recounted less frequently.

Prior qualitative studies have documented the struggle for acceptance among LGBTQ+ Latin Americans, with a focus on the LGBTQ+ individual's experience.[30] But to understand how broader societal attitudes change, it is essential to study not just how LGBTQ+ individuals experience coming out and navigating prejudice, but also how those around them experience someone coming out to them. Interviewing family members and close friends of LGBTQ+ individuals provides us an opportunity to explore and understand how those close to LGBTQ+ individuals think about their acceptance and tolerance – or rejection. Explaining how individuals change their attitudes requires attention to how an LGBTQ+ person's coming out is *received* – how it affects those close to them. In this section, we focus on changes in attitudes of family members and close friends when someone they know comes out. Throughout this section,

---

[29] Of course, there are nuances here. One strategy for "resolving" this tension might be to refuse to believe that a loved one is actually gay.
[30] See, e.g., Armas and Mercedes (2022); Chaux and León (2016); Coppari et al. (2014); Cordero (2018); Corrales and Pecheny (2010); McGee and Kampwirth (2015); Ordóñez, Bulla, Guzmán, and Céspedes (2017); Osorio (2014); Otero Galindo and Meertens (2020). See also movies (Puenzo 2007, 2009), biographies and testimonies from individuals across the region (Bimbi 2017), the biography of a trans child from the mother's point of view (Mansilla 2014), and an award-winning novel based on the life of a college-educated trans sex-worker (Sosa Villada 2019), etc.

we consider both attitudes toward specific individuals (do people accept a loved one who comes out?) and attitudes toward LGBTQ+ communities more broadly (when someone reaches a point of accepting a loved one, is this change also reflected in their broader attitudes about LGBTQ+ rights or people?).

In our conversations, many parents and siblings recounted the process of grappling with their emotions, expectations, and prejudices to accept a son, daughter, or sibling. We observe many cases in which people react to revelations about their loved ones by gradually becoming more tolerant and accepting of LGBTQ+ people. Not everyone accepts their gay and lesbian family members: some resolve the tension in their beliefs by rejecting those who come out to them. But many others gradually moved toward acceptance after some initial processing time.

We also spoke to people who did not experience a fundamental tension in their beliefs: they already held tolerant or accepting attitudes toward LGBTQ+ people. But even when the revelation that a loved one is LGBTQ+ does not change their already-accepting attitudes, it can push them toward further behavioral changes. They begin to see more of a personal stake in LGBTQ+ equality, so they become more active in supporting LGBTQ+ rights and advocating for others to become more tolerant and accepting.

We begin by discussing initial reactions, and then delve into the various paths that people took from rejection to acceptance. We then discuss cases in which a loved one coming out did not change negative attitudes, and the final outcome was rejection.

4.1 Initial Reactions: Shock and Surprise

Some family members and close friends had long suspected their loved one was LGBTQ+. In many cases, parents and siblings told us that they were aware that their sons, daughters, and siblings were gay even before they were told. Others had no idea. This division is not necessarily related to how frequent and close the interactions among individuals were. For instance, we find frequently that a mother "deep down always knew" that her son or daughter was gay while the father "had no clue." In other cases, both parents suspected long before their child came out:

> To be honest with you, we always knew – or we knew long before he told us. My wife realized it before I did, but when she told me, I wasn't surprised. We immediately hugged him when he decided to tell us on Christmas Day. There was no scandal, *nada*. He had already told his brother before us.

In some cases, there was no specific conversation in which the individual came out. Several gay people in their mid-to-late 40s and early 50s told us that they never told their parents or friends they were gay, but they also did not hide it. This is the case of Bárbara, who moved in with her girlfriend Paula without explicitly telling her family and friends that they were a couple:

> I never told her [her mom], but she realized when she saw that Paula and I lived together and that the apartment had only one bedroom with a queen bed. She saw the bed, and her face changed.

A gay man similarly recounted how those close to him in high school knew he was gay, even though he never directly told them:

> I didn't think much about who to tell first. It was obvious that my sister knew. She never told me but made me know, just like my best friend. He didn't tell me, "I know you're gay," but he insisted that I ask out Leo, a boy at school who was gay. We never had a conversation in which I explicitly told them.

Others were taken completely by surprise. And even among those who had an intuition, getting confirmation was often still shocking. As one father who long suspected his son was gay explained:

> Let me be honest, I was very shocked, well not that much because it was kind of obvious, but anyway, it's one thing to think about it and another thing to know it.

For those who had a specific conversation in which a friend, son, daughter, or sibling came out to them, they often do not necessarily remember exactly how they were told, but they do remember where the conversation took place and their reaction: what most of them described as a "shock."

After an initial shock, the next stage that many interviewees described was one of adjustment and processing. Parents and friends described needing time, ranging from minutes to decades, to come to terms with the revelation that someone close to them was gay. Some moved almost immediately from shock to acceptance; for others, it took a long time. And some never fully adjusted to the new information.

Overall, most of our LGBTQ+ interviewees eventually experienced acceptance from their closest friends and family. Many of our interviewees talked about the hurtful things family and friends said when they came out. Yet, they forgave these initial reactions when their family and friends eventually came around.

But even many years after coming out, several still did not have a relationship with certain family members. Eight of our LGBTQ+ interviewees cut ties with family members and friends who did not accept them. Two others lost parents who had never accepted them before passing away, and one spoke of a father who "kind of accepts me, but not really."

What distinguishes those who needed more or less time, and those who eventually expressed acceptance versus rejection?

The patterns we observed in our interviews align with the broader public opinion patterns. Younger people were often the quickest to accept an LGBTQ+ loved one. Often, siblings were more immediately accepting than parents. And those who came out more recently experienced more immediate acceptance than those who came out many decades ago.

Among parents, those who were secular, educated, and living in urban areas were the most likely to accept their children's sexuality; parents who were religious, less educated, and living in rural areas were less likely to accept their children's sexuality.

We also observe gender differences consistent with the public opinion patterns. As we saw in Section 2, on average, women hold more tolerant and accepting views than men toward LGBTQ+ communities. And in interviews, we found that men were more likely to reject their LGBTQ+ relatives than women. In fact, among the set of families we spoke with, all of the individuals who fully rejected an LGBTQ+ family member were fathers or brothers.[31]

For those who were not immediately accepting, but who came around over time, what did the process look like?

4.2 Paths to Acceptance

Not all coming out stories involved a fundamental tension in beliefs: if someone already holds positive – or at least ambivalent – attitudes about gay people, and a loved one comes out to them as gay, there is no conflict to resolve.

But even for those who didn't hold negative views about LGBTQ+ identities, it was often a process to accept the individual and adjust to the revelation that someone close to them was gay. This dynamic was most pronounced among parents. For many, one of the biggest challenges was coming to terms with the idea that their children might never get married or have kids. The challenge here was twofold: parents struggled with reenvisioning the kind of future their child would have; and they were also grappling with what their child's sexuality meant for their own identity – often, whether they would become a grandparent; but also more generally, what it meant to be the parent of someone gay.

---

[31] Of course, there are also women who reject LGBTQ+ friends or family; they just did not appear in our sample. Note as well that finding individuals who rejected a loved one is particularly difficult – in addition to the challenge of identifying such individuals, many would not wish to speak about the issue. Hence, we relied on accounts from those who had been rejected, or from other family members who remained in contact with both their LGBTQ+ relative and the family member who rejected them.

The mother of a well-known gay activist in Argentina told us that a couple of months ago she "came out as a mother of a gay son" for the first time. She was telling us that most people who know her and the family know that her son is gay. Her son has been out for years and is a visible and famous gay activist. Most people who know her know about her gay son. But, this year, she began participating in a craft group that meets once a week, and while crafting and talking about their families, she started talking about her son. Someone asked if he was married and had a family. She said no, and the person commented he'd better hurry or he would not have kids. This comment was not an unusual one, even from a stranger. What was interesting was the mother's response:

> I told her that my son was gay and he did not want to have a family. It was the first time that I talked with strangers about my son's sexuality. First, I felt strange; I had never come out as the mother of a gay son. Then I felt relief like my son was not a criminal; there was nothing to hide.

Even among friends, there was a dynamic of working through what a friend's sexuality meant about their own identity. Friends often described reflecting on their own masculinity, femininity, and sexuality after a close friend came out to them. As one male interviewee said, "What does it say about me that my best friend is gay? Am I gay?" Or as a woman whose best friend came out as lesbian remarked, "After discovering my friend likes women, I began thinking about us – 'Does she like me? Do I like her?'" For some, even simple activities like sleeping over at the friend's house "became a little more weird." As one interviewee told us, after her best friend told her she was gay, sharing the same bed for sleepovers (something they had done for decades) suddenly "felt different."

But over time, the majority of family and friends in our study "made peace" with their sons, daughters, siblings, and friends' sexuality. Although at the beginning many of them thought information about their family and friends' sexual orientations was life-changing, they began thinking that not much had changed. They "knew" and "loved" this individual for so long that they "kind of know them." When friends and family begin accepting that not much has changed or will change, a new relationship embracing acceptance emerges.

Additionally, we frequently observe changes in broader attitudes and behavior regarding LGBTQ+ equality, as people move from acceptance to more active support. Often, people who were already tolerant (or even fully accepting) begin to see more of a personal stake in the equal treatment of LGBTQ+ communities, upon learning that someone they love belongs to the community. Some of them become more active in speaking out and promoting tolerance and acceptance among others. E.g., they might speak out publicly in support of LGBTQ+ rights, get involved in some activism, and begin attending gay pride parades to show solidarity. In most cases, they do not become activists or even proactively make statements about gay rights; but when someone else expresses disapproval towards the sexual orientation of their friend or family member, they will speak up to voice their support.

***

The path to acceptance was generally rockier for those who held negative views about LGBTQ+ people more broadly. Yet many did eventually reach a point of accepting their loved one's identity.

When a loved one came out to someone who held intolerant attitudes towards LGBTQ+ people, it created a tension in their beliefs. This tension came up most often for those who were highly religious and viewed LGBTQ+ identities as sinful. But for some, their long-standing relationship and sense that their LGBTQ+ loved one was a good person pushed them to adjust their attitudes. They might not become fully supportive of LGBTQ+ rights, but we saw many examples where these individuals became more tolerant.

One illustrative account of change came from Sabrina, a religious woman whose lifelong friend Marina came out to her as a lesbian. Sabrina and Marina grew up together, going to the same schools, living in the same neighborhood, "sharing a life together."

Sabrina did not grow up in an especially religious household, but her husband did. When Sabrina met him, she also became more religious and together they created a religious household, similar to the one he grew up in. They attend church every Sunday and participate actively in the life of the church. With their church community, they have participated in mobilizations against gay rights and abortion.

But after Marina came out, Sabrina did not reject her, maintaining that "She is my best friend." When we asked her about how she thinks about her friend being gay, she responded that she doesn't seek to impose her religious views on others.

Sabrina and her husband both maintain a close relationship with Marina, whom they describe with love and respect. After Marina came out to them, they continued to participate in anti-abortion rallies. But they no longer attend the rallies against same-sex marriage.

Reflecting on their decision to accept their friend, Sabrina and her husband told us about a deeply difficult time they had gone through before Marina came out. Sabrina was pregnant, but they knew that the pregnancy would either end in a stillbirth or a newborn who would die only a few hours after birth. They decided to go through with the pregnancy because of their religious views.

Many people in their lives who did not share their religious views were highly critical of this decision.

Sabrina's husband reflected with us about how he would never forget Marina's attitude as they went through this "life-challenging" event – her acceptance towards their religious beliefs.

> When we decided to have the baby, many people got angry with us, mainly with me. Sabrina's family treated us like crazy. How could we suffer so much? Why do we choose to suffer, to continue with the pregnancy? Sabrina's mom stopped talking to us for a while. On the other hand, Marina never questioned us. I'm sure she thought we were crazy, but she accompanied us and never said anything. I will never forget that.

In conversations with other religious individuals who have gay friends or family, the language of "not imposing" their views on others came up frequently. Many said that they haven't changed how they personally feel about issues such as same-sex marriage, homosexuality, or trans rights, but that it doesn't bother them if others don't share their views. For Sabrina and her husband, it's not clear whether they have changed their beliefs about the morality of homosexuality. But their decision to stop attending anti-gay rights rallies is a clear sign that they have become more tolerant.

We also learned of friends and family who, after a loved one came out, decided to stop attending events with people who make openly anti-gay comments, or would leave when comments were made. One man recounted a story of a barbecue he attended with friends after a soccer game. The group had been holding this postgame barbecue for decades. But then, at one of the barbecues, a friend of a friend from the rival team began saying negative things about gay men. One of the friends, whose brother was gay, very visibly stood up and left, saying "I'd better go or I'll beat him up." The man who had made the comments was told that the brother of the one who left was gay. One of the friends present at the incident described anti-gay comments as "unacceptable." And after this incident, the postgame barbecues continued, but there was no more trash-talking gay people at them.

4.3 Rejection

Not everyone who is intolerant towards LGBTQ+ people adopts new attitudes, beliefs, or behaviors in response to a loved one coming out. Some hold steadfast in their anti-LGBTQ+ attitudes and refuse to accept their children, siblings, and friends' sexual orientations and identities. Rather than reject their previously held beliefs about LGBTQ+ identities, they reject the individual who comes out to them.

In some cases, rejection takes the form of complete ostracism – acting as if a person is dead due to their sexual orientation and cutting off all contact. In others, the individual might seek to maintain some contact but forbid any mentioning of sexual orientation – in essence, maintaining a sense of denial around their LGBTQ+ contact's identity and demanding that their LGBTQ+ contact facilitate that denial.

Of course, parents who chose to reject their sons and daughters due to their sexual orientation were generally less interested in discussing the matter with us than those who eventually accepted their children. Moreover, many of our LGBTQ+ interviewees had lost contact with those that rejected them; therefore, it was hard to find them. Instead, we generally had to rely on accounts from those that they rejected, or from mutual contacts (e.g., a sibling who remains in contact with the parents that rejected their other child).

In most cases, the parents and siblings who rejected their LGBTQ+ family member were deeply religious and envisioned their son's, daughter's, or sibling's identity as both a choice and a sin. They could not forgive or understand how someone they raised could "choose" something they viewed as sinful.

One of the barriers to attitude change among highly religious individuals was their involvement in a religious *community*. Religion is not merely a belief system; it also constitutes a social identity. For many, their place in the church forms an important part of their identity that would be difficult to walk away from. Within their community, they are exposed regularly to denouncements of LGBTQ+ identification as a sin. Some might feel compelled to visibly distance themselves from a friend or family member who comes out, as a way of maintaining their own identity and place in a religious community.

Religious parents who reject their sons or daughters' sexual orientations end up rejecting their sons and daughters altogether. Most of them acted as if they had died, and some of them told us that their parents talked about them as if they had been killed the day they came out. Siblings sometimes, often clandestinely, continue a relationship. And in some cases, mothers, without their husband's knowledge, continue seeing their sons and daughters or sending them money and food. We met once with a mother through her daughter who still has contact with her homosexual brother. The mother told us that she "hated" that her son was gay, but he was still her son, and she missed him. Her husband would not forgive her if she ever talked to him again, and thus, she frequently cooked him his favorite food and sent it to him through her daughter. She said that if her husband found out, he would "kill her."

Stories of rejection do not end well. In some cases, we learned about LGBTQ+ people who chose to end their lives. In others, we talked with some who had carried considerable trauma due to the rejection and the abrupt end of their belonging to a solid religious community they had known all their lives. Others abandon their families and communities and build a new life, usually in a new city or country.

4.4 Trans Coming Out Experiences

The examples described above highlight the process by which people react to learning that someone close to them is gay, lesbian, or bisexual. Considering trans coming out experiences, there are some major differences in the frequency with which transgender individuals are accepted or rejected. And people often take more time to adjust to the revelation of one's transgender identity than to the revelation of one's sexuality.

But in our conversations with transgender individuals and their friends and family, we observe a very similar process of reacting to this new information and either reconsidering one's views about transgender people to move towards acceptance, or holding on to intolerant views and rejecting their transgender friend or relative.

As was the case for LGB coming out experiences, some people knew or suspected that an individual they knew was transgender before that individual came out to them. In fact, in some instances, a friend of a transgender person knew before that individual had even privately come to this realization about themselves.

In one interview with a trans woman, she told us that one of her teachers in high school privately asked her if she preferred to be called by another name when they were alone. (At the time, she had a name and pronouns identified as male.) At the time, the individual was just confused. She was not even alarmed that something was obvious. It was only when she came out in college that she began thinking about that teacher and her "compassion towards her" as she was attending a private Catholic school where trans students were not accepted.

Public discussion and recognition of transgender identities is relatively new; especially prior to the internet and social media, many people did not have access to any information about transgender people. Thus, it is not surprising that in some cases a sympathetic teacher might knew before the individual in question has found the words to describe their gender identity.

***

Across these interviews, whether the subject was sexuality or gender identity, some consistent patterns emerged. Often, especially among those who held particularly negative attitudes towards LGBTQ+ individuals prior to a loved one coming out, the process of attitude change was extremely slow. Many of these individuals would register as non-responsive to contact treatments in a well-designed experiment like those conducted by Broockman and Kalla. But eventually, many of them are indeed responsive when that contact is sustained and is with someone with whom they already had strong ties, before learning the individual was LGBTQ+.

The experience of learning that a close friend or family member is LGBTQ+ doesn't eliminate all the other predictors of attitudes towards LGBTQ+ people and rights. Sometimes it can counter demographic or social characteristics that would make one less likely to accept; but in other cases, those characteristics can blunt the process of acceptance, or prevent it from even starting. Looking across the cases in our interviews, patterns emerge that are consistent with the public opinion literature on predictors of tolerance and acceptance: mothers were more likely to accept their children than fathers; religious individuals were often more reluctant to accept LGBTQ+ people than those who were nonreligious. But that is not to say that the outcomes were predetermined. For example, the case of Sabrina and her friend Marina illustrated how personal contact created cross-pressures for a highly religious individual, eventually settling into an outcome of increased tolerance.

Grappling with the revelation of a loved one's sexuality or gender identity is a unique and particularly powerful experience. But there are other forms of personal interaction and contact that can also change attitudes. In the next sections, we turn to other forms of contact and exposure that, even if less intense and sustained, also contributed to the growth of tolerance and acceptance.

5 Changing Behavior before Attitudes: Economic Incentives for Tolerance

Studying the process by which people react to a loved one coming out, we saw many instances in which people gradually changed their beliefs and attitudes. Then, once their attitudes changed, some people subsequently changed their behavior.

But change does not always occur on a linear trajectory from attitudes to behavior. Sometimes, attitude change comes *after* behavioral change. A prime example of this dynamic comes from the tourism and hospitality industry, where economic dynamics brought workers increasingly into contact with openly gay and lesbian patrons. Drawing on extensive interviews with tourism and hospitality workers in Buenos Aires, we show how economic incentives led customer-facing workers to change their behavior at work – *acting* more tolerant – while still holding intolerant views. These behavioral changes eventually led to attitudinal changes as well, following repeated positive interactions with LGBTQ+ customers. Workers who initially *acted* more tolerant eventually *became* more tolerant as a result.

During the 1990s, neoliberal reforms led many cities in Latin America to experience a consumption boom. Capital cities in the region experienced urban renewal, the construction of massive shopping malls, and the emergence of clubs, saunas, bookstores, coffee shops, and restaurants that exclusively catered to gay and lesbian customers (Insausti & Ben 2023). Capitalism led to the integration of gay and lesbian individuals with economic power. LGBTQ+ activists also leveraged the opening up of Latin American economies during the early 1990s as an opportunity to combat discrimination and strengthen the presence of their community. Domestic and international gay spending contributed to combating discrimination and affirming gay identity (Encarnación 2011). Low prices led to a boom in international tourism, including from international gay travelers. Many of these gay travelers spent substantial amounts of money, transforming some capital cities in the region into hubs for gay tourism. Local business owners also saw an opportunity to cater to families with double incomes and no kids who were eager to spend their disposable income.

In the case of gay and lesbian individuals who could afford to spend money on housing, education, entertainment, and traveling, their consumption behavior led to the opening of new markets and businesses designed to cater to this population. Those who could afford to live in up-and-coming neighborhoods, eat out in restaurants, and enjoy the nightlife and entertainment found in big cities became an attractive group to target. Whereas there were always people who did not like "the gays," they agreed to provide services to them when they found out they were good customers – that they were good clients who paid on time, did not make any problems, and were good tippers.

This dynamic of consumption-led acceptance is illustrated in changes in the behavior of waiters in Latin American cities. Waiters in the region are long-term employees, many of whom have had professional careers in waiting tables. Most waiters are employed in restaurants and coffee shops in the cities but do not live in the area. In several interviews we conducted with waiters, they recounted how they changed their minds about serving gay and lesbian customers. In the beginning, they disliked serving gay and lesbian couples. They were rude to them. Yet, the street rumor began to spread: "These people spend a lot of money, buy good wine, indulge in ordering multiple plates, and give good tips when served with grace." Waiters began changing their strategy, mostly to get tips.

Mario, a veteran waiter at a cafeteria in Buenos Aires, describes this change from rejection to tolerance:

"I never liked *trolos* (gay despective). At first, I didn't even want to serve them. When I saw them sitting at a table, I acted as if I hadn't seen them, waited for them to leave, and when they stayed, I served them in a bad mood. Sometimes, I even served them a wrong order on purpose. It was fucked. One of the younger guys (waiters) was cool and took good care of them. The ball began to spread, and several came and sat at the tables that belonged to this one. Suddenly, we saw they ordered the most expensive dishes on the menu, drank more than one bottle of expensive wine, and left 15 or 20 percent as a tip. And well, I'm not stupid. I started to be "the tolerant one," and things improved. They always treated me well, spent a lot, and left good tips, especially the Yankees. Now they don't bother me."

Mario's testimony illustrates a pattern we found in several interviews with service industry employees. In short, they changed their behavior to be economically rewarded. We did not find evidence that management forced waiters to serve gay and lesbian couples or that they engaged in any kind of diversity training for their staff. The most straightforward market logic led to changes in the service industry: if you wanted to make more money, you were better off serving gay customers. Whereas changes in attitudes began as "acting as if" waiters and hostesses did not notice or mind the sexual orientations of their customers; eventually, by "acting as if," they became, in many cases, more tolerant and even accepting of differences.

Hotel staffers offered similar testimonies, echoing how direct contact with and economic benefit from LGBTQ+ tourists led to eventual attitude changes. Latin American big cities benefited from global LGBTQ+ tourism during the 90s. Gay tourists looked to travel to places where they could feel safe and avoid harassment. Identifying hotels where they would be welcome was vital. A proliferation of gay and lesbian travel guides provided information on which cities were safe and welcoming, with thriving gay communities. They recommended specific hotels and restaurants that were frequented by LGBTQ+ clientele in many countries, including Brazil, Argentina, Mexico, Costa Rica, Guatemala, and Honduras. Buenos Aires in particular was often highlighted as a gay-friendly destination – according to one guide, "the gay capital city of South America" (Gmünder 2000); another guide declared that "Buenos Aires is probably only second to Rio de Janeiro (Brazil) when it comes to gay nightlife" (Angelo & Bain 1997).

In our conversations with hotel managers in Buenos Aires, those who had been working in the industry since the 1990s described a change over time in how gay and lesbian tourists were treated. A 43-year-old receptionist of a big chain hotel in the city told us that challenges sometimes arose when older receptionists needed to assign rooms with a queen bed to a gay or lesbian couple:

> See, the problem with gays was with older people. It made them uncomfortable having two guys or two girls sharing a queen bed. It didn't matter to us (the young people).

We frequently heard accounts of how the business incentive drove some more intolerant workers to treat gay and lesbian customers better, even if they didn't like them:

> We treat them well. People pretend everything is okay because it suits them; because it is a business. It bothers some (workers), it doesn't bother others, I think it is becoming more common and less annoying.

And over time, many workers who initially took issue with gay clientele became more tolerant. A veteran worker, who was going to retire that year and was currently in a managerial post, described a change from profound dislike to almost acceptance:

> At first I preferred to think that they were friends traveling together. I gave them separate beds and then the maids came and told me that they had put the beds together, I didn't like it. Now it bothers me less, well, the truth is that it doesn't bother me.

In our conversations, it was clear that the constant interaction with gay tourists changed this manager's perspective. He mentioned – like Mario, the waiter – the fact that they were good clients: they were respectful to staff, paid on time, and gave good tips.

In sum, our interviews and informal conversations with waiters, hostesses, and hotel workers – most of them with high school diplomas and self-identified as working-class – point to another path towards tolerance and acceptance. As homosexuality became more openly acknowledged and economic markets opened up, there were monetary incentives to treat gay and lesbian customers well. And repeated positive interactions with these gay and lesbian customers – interactions in which workers benefited financially and were treated with respect – often gradually changed their views of the LGBTQ+ community.

As in the cases of friends and family coming out, the path to tolerance and acceptance here relies on some general human tendencies of attitude change that travel beyond Latin America; but the circumstances that brought about these attitude-changing interactions were more context-specific. It was the particular economic environment that emerged in late-20th century Latin America that generated these economic incentives to first treat gay customers with respect; and then, more general tendencies to change one's beliefs to align with one's experiences led to many hospitality workers adopting more tolerant and accepting attitudes.

6 Pop Culture and Representation

In addition to direct interactions with LGBTQ+ individuals, another key factor in shaping attitudes is the indirect exposure provided by popular culture and the media.

Up to this point, we have focused on face-to-face interactions with LGBTQ+ individuals. But scholars at the intersection of psychology and communications studies have argued that media consumption provides "the illusion of face-to-face relationship" (Horton & Richard Wohl 1956: 215). Hence, exposure to LGBTQ+ individuals and characters in the media can operate similarly to in-person contact: media exposure contributes to the formation of beliefs about minorities (Allport 1954; Entman & Rojecki 2001) and negative stereotypes can be challenged by the affective parasocial relationships viewers develop with television personas (Schiappa et al. 2006).

Over time, LGBTQ+ representation in the media has expanded. Ayoub and Garretson (2017: 1064) note that the number of lesbian, gay, and bisexual characters in American TV shows more than tripled between the late 1980s and 1995 – and continued to increase since. And their survey of 180 LGBT organizations across 47 European countries pointed to a similar expansion of media representation across the continent – described by respondents as an "explosive turn in the early 1990s." Representation has often started with gay male characters; over time, the stories told include lesbian, bisexual, and trans characters.

In Latin America as well, representation has grown and expanded over the past few decades.

6.1 Representation in Latin American Media

Before the third wave of democratization, positive LGBTQ+ representation in mainstream media was virtually unheard of even in the most progressive Latin American countries. But in May 1984, one year after Argentina's return to democracy, the influential gay activist Carlos Jáuregui made history with an appearance on the cover of *Siete Días* magazine. The cover (pictured in Fig. 11) featured the title "The risk of being homosexual in Argentina." Jáuregui and fellow activist Raúl Soria's "loving embrace was the first time two gay men freely and openly declared their homosexuality in the national media" (Lipsky 2021).

One year later, in 1985, another gay activist, Zelmar Acevedo, appeared in one of the most-watched political programs in Argentina: "A solas con Hugo Guerrero Marthineitz." Acevedo had been an active participant of the *Frente para la Liberación Homosexual* (Front for Homosexual Liberation)

Figure 11 Carlos Jáuregui on the cover of *Siete Días*, May 1984.

in the 70s and was the then-vice-president of the *Comunidad Homosexual Argentina* (Argentine Homosexual Community). He was invited to appear in the program to discuss his new book: *"Homosexualidad: hacia la destrucción de los mitos"* ("Homosexuality: towards the destruction of myths"). The program, which started at midnight, had a record audience, and it was discussed for weeks after it aired. Guerrero Marthineitz won the most prestigious television award that year, the Martin Fierro.

A pivotal moment in the history of gay politics in Argentina came on a TV drama. In 1992, the blockbuster show *Zona de Riesgo* broke new ground by featuring a gay couple. In an episode airing close to midnight, the show portrayed two men kissing each other. Two famous straight actors portrayed the gay couple. Gerardo Romano, one of the actors, later said the show was successful because it was truly believable. They portrayed what he defined as a "history of gay love as if it was hetero[sexual love]."[32] It was, in that sense, the height of respectability politics: for straight audience members, *Zona de Riesgo* was portraying gay characters as "just like you" (Guiñazú 2024).

For some audience members, this might have been the first time they saw someone gay as relatable. Presenting images of LGBTQ+ people to non-LGBTQ+ people that portray them as being "just like you" can contribute

---

[32] América TV (2021), URL: www.youtube.com/watch?v=sppx7WwELzk.

to de-othering. This can help people begin to accept LGBTQ+ people, as perceived similarity breeds empathy (see, e.g., Hoffman 2000: 208–209).

But this form of representation also has downsides. It can create and reinforce divisions within the LGBTQ+ community: those whose presentation, lifestyle, or other characteristics fall outside the norms that a respectability politics strategy emulates can be pushed "to the margins" (Moscowitz 2013: 133). And some recent empirical work has questioned the notion that these strategies are even very effective in increasing public support (Jones 2022).

In the intervening decades, LGBTQ+ representation on television has expanded well beyond a single gay couple. No longer a dichotomy between straight-passing gay characters or demeaning stereotypes, media representations have moved towards recognizing the complexity and individuality of LGBTQ+ identities. And while early representations generally included only gay men, we now see increasing portrayals of other identities: lesbian, bisexual, transgender. Just last year, an Argentine bio series documenting the life of "trans icon" (De Paulo 2017) Cris Miró was released. The show, *Cris Miró (Ella)*, documents Miró's life and society's reaction to a trans celebrity in the mid-to-late 1990s.

In other countries, too, representation has expanded and evolved over the years. The first gay character in Brazilian telenovelas appeared in 1970, on the show *Assim Na Terra Como No Céu*. The character, Rodolfo Augusto, was a costume designer portrayed as an "effeminate caricature" with an "indication of asexuality" (Junior & Gonçalves 2017: 119). In 1981, the Brazilian show *Brilhante* moved towards a more humanized and sympathetic portrayal of a gay character. The portrayal in *Brilhante* avoided the stereotypes and caricatures of earlier portrayals, though it still relied on subtext and suggestion in place of directly addressing the character's sexuality.

In 1988, Brazil was the sixth country in television history to feature a show with a queer female character (after the United States, Japan, Australia, United Kingdom, and Germany).[33] In the groundbreaking 1988 Brazilian telenovela *Vale Tudo*, the character Laís, played by Cristina Prochaska, represented one of the earliest instances of LGBTQ+ visibility on national television. As an openly lesbian woman, Laís's character was revolutionary in a time when such portrayals were nearly absent from mainstream media. Though her storyline was secondary and her relationship with her partner received limited attention, her presence significantly challenged the norms of the time. At the beginning

---

[33] From www.lezwatchtv.com/, Database of Queer Female, Non-Binary, & Transgender TV. Accessed April 17, 2025.

of the telenovela, Lais had been in a relationship with another woman for 12 years, and they ran a successful business together.

By the turn of the 21st century, LGBTQ+ representation had evolved and expanded in Brazil; yet still no telenovela had ever shown a gay kiss. In 2005, the novela *America* included in its script a kiss between two gay characters. The scene was filmed, but after negative reception in focus groups, it was discarded and never shown. It was not until 2010 – 40 years after the first appearance of an LGBTQ+ character – that a Brazilian telenovela finally showed a gay kiss (between two female characters, on *Love and Revolution*) (Junior & Gonçalves 2017: 120).

Of course, not all media portrayals are positive, even today. And the trajectory of media representation is often not linear. In 1999, the show *La vida en el espejo* marked a significant advancement in the portrayal of LGBTQ+ characters within Mexican soap operas. Unlike its predecessors, this soap opera featured a diverse cast of gay characters whose storylines explored themes of love, acceptance, and the complexities of family dynamics, offering a more nuanced representation of their experiences. Including these characters indicated a changing cultural landscape in Mexico, as the late 1990s saw a growing willingness to confront social issues and challenge traditional norms in mainstream media. Yet, examining Mexican masculinity in soap operas, Tate (2013) shows that *telenovelas* produced after *La Vida* continued to enforce a narrative of heteronormativity. In *Velo de novia* (2003–04), *Rubí* (2004–05), and *La fea más bella* (2006–07), "gay characters work in the beauty or design industries, are extremely effeminate, and behave (and are treated) as if they are one of the girls" (Tate 2013: 244). Even when some soap operas portray the realistic and complex lives of LGBTQ+ individuals, others continue portraying stereotypical images that do not force spectators to question their assumptions about LGBTQ+ individuals.

Today, the frequency and nature of LGBTQ+ representation varies widely across Latin America. Between 2002 and 2019, 67 prime-time telenovelas featuring LGBTQ+ characters aired in Brazil. In El Salvador, there was only one (Gulesci et al. 2024). But amid the globalization of media, we see increasing diffusion across countries. Even in countries that produce few to no shows or movies featuring LGBTQ+ characters, people are often exposed to representations from other countries' productions. *Cris Miró (Ella)* is an Argentine production; but with distribution from HBO Max and TNT, it received a widespread international release, airing elsewhere in Latin America, as well as in the United States and Europe. *Una mujer fantástica*, a 2017 Chilean movie about a trans woman, was also widely distributed – opening to international acclaim and winning the Academy Award for Best Foreign Language Film along with major awards in Mexico, Brazil, Cuba, Spain, and Germany.

6.2 How Does Representation Shape Attitudes?

How has the proliferation of LGBTQ+ characters in television shows shaped attitudes? Prior research has found evidence that increased exposure to sympathetic portrayals of gay and lesbian characters fosters greater acceptance (see, e.g., Garretson 2015; Schiappa et al. 2006). But pioneering representation of minority groups is never met with universal acceptance. In some cases, LGBTQ+ storylines have garnered negative reactions and backlash. When Rede Globo, the largest TV network in Brazil, launched a 2015 soap opera featuring a lesbian couple, a conservative backlash led to record-low viewership and calls for boycotting a cosmetics company that sponsored the show (Gomes & Cantu 2023: 268).

Gulesci et al. (2024) analyzed the introduction of LGBTQ+ characters in telenovelas across 14 countries in Latin America and the Caribbean and found that, if anything, expanding representation of LGBTQ+ characters yielded a short-term shift *away* from tolerance. The authors find that the effect is driven by comedies rather than dramas, and they note that the comedic shows in the sample leaned more heavily on caricatures when portraying LGBTQ+ individuals – in stark contrast to the sympathetic and relatable portrayals that scholars have highlighted in arguments for how representation can foster acceptance (Schiappa et al. 2006).

And it's not just a numbers game; even a single major portrayal can have an effect. Two careful studies of attitudes in the US found that the TV show *Will & Grace* was so influential that it significantly improved attitudes towards LGBTQ+ communities, particularly among young viewers (Garretson 2015; Schiappa et al. 2006).

Moreover, expanding representation can have downstream effects on tolerance and acceptance that quasi-experimental designs don't capture. Quasi-experiments (such as Garretson 2015, which leveraged the timing of surveys just before and just after major media portrayals) are well-designed for capturing the reactions of non-LGBTQ+ people to expanding representation. They help to answer the question, does exposure to positive portrayals in the media change the attitudes of those who have negative perceptions of LGBTQ+ people or who have little exposure to LGBTQ+ people in their day-to-day lives? But this is not the only path by which representation can enhance tolerance and acceptance. Another important dimension is how these representations affect LGBTQ+ viewers.

For LGBTQ+ viewers, media representation can help individuals understand themselves and envision a life where they could live openly. And to the extent that media representation helps LGBTQ+ individuals come out, it enables the dynamics presented in Section 4: as more LGBTQ+ people come out, more non-LGBTQ+ people experience learning that someone close to them is LGBTQ+ and move towards greater tolerance and acceptance.

Indeed, in our interviews, several participants mentioned the "huge impact" of seeing someone like them on television and in printed media. It was after seeing or listening to someone self-identify as homosexual on television or print that some of our interviewees began thinking about their own sexual identity.

One of our interviewees recalled watching Zelmar Acevedo's appearance on Guerrero Marthineitz's program in 1985. He watched the program with his parents and described "understanding for the first time that I was like Acevedo, homosexual." The interviewee's mother also remembered watching the program and thinking her son might have been like Acevedo.

Increased media representation and access to social media is especially vital for individuals who are not often exposed to LGBTQ+ individuals, particularly those who live in rural areas – as was the case for the gay man who recounted his realization upon watching Zelmar Acevedo on TV. Our in-depth interviews document the effect that the public appearance of these characters has had on those who identify as gay and trans, as well as on those who did not know much about sexual and gender minorities. Many of our interviewees, both those who identify as LGBTQ+ and those who do not, clearly remember the first time they saw a gay character, whether in print or on television.

7 Demographic Changes and the Nuclear Family

The preceding sections describe how contact and exposure – both direct and indirect – have contributed to attitude change in Latin America. But there are also other macro-level factors that facilitated the trend towards greater tolerance and acceptance. The late 20th century brought many changes to societies in Latin America – including a gradual shift in family structures. In many Latin American countries, divorce only became legal in the late 20th century.[34] And in many cases where it was legal earlier, its use was restricted to specific circumstances (e.g., only in cases of adultery).

But even before divorce was legalized in many countries, families were changing. Consider Brazil, where divorce became legal in 1977. In Mala

---

[34] The last country in the region to legalize divorce, Chile, only did so in 2004.

Htun's (2003) book *Sex and the State*, she reports a steady rise in marital separations since the 1950s, with the rate doubling in the 1950s, tripling in the 1960s, and doubling again in the 1970s to early 1980s. By 1985, marital separations were more than sixteen times as common as they had been in 1950.

And since the 1980's, Latin America has seen a substantial increase in divorces, children born out of wedlock, and assembled families across all social classes (Ben & Insausti 2021; Hiller 2017).

The rise of divorce and nontraditional family structures played two key roles in shifting attitudes towards LGBTQ+ people. On a societal level, the decline of traditional marriage as a social institution fostered more openness to alternative family structures of many kinds – including same-sex relationships. And on an individual level, first-hand experiences with divorce often helped parents come to accept their children.

7.1 Changing Social Institutions: Marriage and Family Structures

Ben and Insausti (2021: 11) observe that "in the last decades, traditional heterosexual marriage lost ground as a social institution." The late 20th and early 21st century was a time of upheaval in marriage and family structures. Before same-sex marriage was on the policy agenda in any Latin American country, the traditional idea of the nuclear family was being challenged from many other angles. More marriages were ending in divorce (García & Rojas 2001); single-person households became more common (Arriagada 2006); and even among those in stable long-term relationships, more couples chose to cohabitate but not get married (Esteve et al. 2012; Ramm 2016) or not to have children (Arriagada 2006).

Alongside these changes came an increase in " 'assembled families' where one or both parents have children from a previous union" (Ben & Insausti 2021: 11). Thus, not only did the possibility of impermanence in marital relationships become normalized; alternative arrangements for parenting also grew more widespread. These include arrangements where a child might be raised by a single parent, or might have more than two parental figures in their lives – both a father and a step-father, a mother and a step-mother.

In recent decades, society transitioned from often rigid norms that dictated what a family should look like, and grew accustomed to more flexible and fluid definitions of familial relationships. By 2006, 27 percent of Chileans said that marriage was an "outdated institution" – nearly doubling support for this idea from 15 percent in 1990. This sentiment was shared by 29 percent of Argentines, 28 percent of Mexicans, 24 percent of Uruguayans, 21 percent of

Brazilians, and 20 percent of Peruvians.[35] The decline of traditional marriage as a social institution created an opening for greater social acceptance of same-sex relationships and for policy advances on same-sex marriage.

The legalization of same-sex marriage was certainly not an inevitable outcome of the broader changes in family structures. As we will discuss in greater detail in the next chapter, the fight for same-sex marriage is ongoing in many countries; and in those countries where same-sex couples have won the right to marry, those marriage rights were only attainable after years of dedicated efforts among activists. But the decline of the traditional nuclear family as a social institution was also an important factor in progress towards marriage equality and social acceptance. Same-sex marriage had fewer hurdles to overcome in a "culture where heterosexual informal unions and divorce had become mainstream" (Ben & Insausti 2021: 160, citing Hiller 2017).

Legalizing adoption by same-sex couples similarly became more feasible in a context where many children were being raised in households with a set of parents other than their two biological parents. Just like same-sex marriage faced fewer hurdles as divorce became more mainstream, same-sex adoption faced fewer hurdles as alternative parenting arrangements became more mainstream. As people grow more accustomed to diverse family structures, they can more easily envision different ways of raising a child beyond a household with their biological mother and father.

Consider Chile. In 1960, only 16 percent of children in Chile were born outside of marriage; by 2010, that figure had increased to 68 percent (Salinas 2011). Many unmarried parents cohabitate; but an estimated 30 percent of children born from 2006 to 2009 were not living with their biological father in 2010 (Cuesta & Reynolds 2022). And between 1990 and 2006, the proportion of Chileans agreeing that "children need a home with both a father and a mother" declined from 92 percent to 75 percent (Esteve et al. 2012). By 2012, 63 percent of Chileans said that single parents could raise children just as well as married couples.[36] Of course, this does not automatically translate to equal support for same-sex parents. Support for the idea that children can thrive with same-sex parents still lags far behind: in 2017, only 37 percent agreed that same-sex couples can raise a child just as well as a heterosexual couple

---

[35] World Values Survey (WVS), 2005–2009 wave. The countries listed here are the only Latin American countries included in the WVS 2005–2009 wave. Note that more recent waves of the WVS did not include this question.

[36] Data from International Social Survey Programme 2012: Family and Changing Gender Roles IV.

(41 percent disagreed). But this is up dramatically from only 26 percent agreement (and 58 percent disagreement) just seven years prior in 2010.[37]

Some of this gap in support for a same-sex couple's ability to raise a child versus a single parent's ability to raise a child likely reflects general prejudices against LGBT people (Why would two moms be less able to raise a child than a single mom? Two dads less able than a single dad?). But some portion of the gap might also be explained by assumptions about gender. When asked about single parents, how often do respondents think of single fathers versus single mothers? When asked about same-sex couples, how often do respondents think of gay male versus lesbian couples? Perhaps people assume that most single parents are single mothers (an accurate assumption – see, e.g., *The Economist* 2023) and believe that women are better equipped to raise children than men; if they think of gay male couples compared to heterosexual couples, the lack of a female parent might depress support. Indeed, when the same 2017 survey asked whether a single heterosexual man should have the same right to adopt a child as a single heterosexual woman, only 49 percent agreed (28 percent disagreed) – highlighting these gendered beliefs about who is more suited to child-rearing.[38] Breaking down support for adoption by gay male versus lesbian couples, we do see a gap – though it's rather small, with 38 percent supporting lesbian couples' right to adopt (42 percent opposed) versus 34 percent supporting gay male couples' right to adopt (45 percent opposed).[39]

While significant obstacles remain for same-sex couples' right to marry and to adopt children in many Latin American and Caribbean countries, the region has made substantial progress in just 15 years. This progress reflects, in part, public opinion shifts in the wake of changing social norms. Latin America has undergone a long-term process in which traditional heterosexual marriage has declined – both in its frequency and its role as a social institution. People have become more open to alternative family structures, creating an opening for gay rights activists to push for marriage and adoption rights. And these legal victories have further contributed to social acceptance. This effect is particularly prominent among parents, many of whom became more accepting of their child's sexual orientation upon learning that their child might still marry and have children – a dynamic that came up frequently in our interviews.

---

[37] Data comes from the *Centro de Estudios Públicos*, survey waves 64 (Jun–Jul 2010) and 79 (Apr–May 2017).

[38] In addition to gendered beliefs about who is better able to raise a child, these survey responses might also reflect heightened concerns about potential male child predators versus female child predators.

[39] *Centro de Estudios Públicos*, wave 79.

7.2 Parental Acceptance: Expectations and Reenvisioning the Future

Parents develop certain expectations for what their children's lives will look like. Some of these expectations relate to shared experiences: a mother might look forward to her daughter having children so that they can share in the experience of motherhood. Other expectations center around the parent's future role and identity, such as becoming a grandparent. These expectations, often developing when a child is very young (or even before a child is born) can be difficult to let go of; and these expectations around one's future family often came up as an obstacle to acceptance in our interviews.

The demographic changes discussed in the previous section helped many to come around to eventual acceptance. In some cases, it was a matter of being open to the idea that their child could get married and have children, just not in the way they had originally imagined. In other cases, personal experience with divorce prepared parents to reenvision their child's future, just like they had reenvisioned their own future when their marriage ended.

7.2.1 Imagining a Future Family: Challenges to Acceptance

Upon learning that one's child is LGBT, parents often face a challenge of letting go of the future they had once imagined for their child, and replacing it with new ideas about what their child's life and family will look like.

The desire for grandchildren

For many of the parents we interviewed, one of the most difficult aspects of learning their child was gay was the idea that they would never have grandchildren. Parents' loss of their future identity as grandparents appeared systematically in our interviews, as these quotes from three different interviews illustrate:

> Since I had [son's name] I always thought about my grandchildren. I think what bothered me the most, hurt me, about him being homosexual was that I wasn't going to have grandchildren. I didn't like anything about the choice of [son's name], I was afraid of how he was going to suffer for being different, and I think a little bit being selfish, I suffered because I wasn't going to be a grandmother.

> It made me very angry knowing that we were never going to have grandchildren.

> To think that he was going to have a life so different, so far from what I always imagined. What I knew. The worst thing was the loneliness, that we were going to miss out on having a family, and that it would leave us without the miracle that are grandchildren.

These interviews accurately transcribed the anger (*bronca*), and the acute sense of loss that these parents feel when confronted with the possibility that they will not have grandchildren.

Gendered expectations and motherhood

The parents of homosexual sons and daughters alike shared feelings of anger and loss about the idea of never being grandparents. But in the case of daughters, there is an additional gendered dimension: parents reflect on their daughters missing out on what they envisioned as an important – and for some of them vital – experience of womanhood: becoming a mother.[40]

These gendered expectations often center around the idea of having shared experiences between a parent and child of the same gender. The concern over one's daughter missing out on motherhood came up frequently in our interviews with mothers, but not with fathers.

As one mother of a lesbian daughter explained:

> It scared me that she was going to miss motherhood, that she was not going to have children, a family. My belly hurt all the time, imagining her old and alone. She used to annoy me – a lot of anger. I had to do a lot of therapy to calm down and be able to accompany her. In the end, do you know what happened? She got married and has children. She found a woman who is like a man; they used fertilization, and I was able to accompany my daughter during pregnancy and childbirth, and now I take care of my grandchildren. I'm not going to tell you that it was easy. It took me a lot to get used to and understand it at first. Now, here I am. Sometimes, I think about how my grandchildren will not have a dad, but I think about love. They don't have a father, but they have two mothers who love each other very much. And two grandparents.

Similar themes came up in many interviews with mothers of lesbian daughters: that they wanted their daughters to experience motherhood and were saddened by the idea that they might not share this experience. But, in many cases, they did end up having grandchildren, an outcome that led them to greater acceptance of their child's identity. As another mother recounted:

> I always wanted [name] to be a mom. She never had a maternal instinct, she never had the desire either. Paradoxically, it was when she met [wife's name] that they decided to have a family. Nothing turned out as I imagined, but here I am, like any grandmother taking care of my grandchildren.

---

[40] In this regard, it is interesting to note that no parent ever mentioned the fact that their children were missing out on the opportunity to become "fathers." Fatherhood, as opposed to motherhood, did not appear in our interviews – reflecting how ingrained social norms about motherhood are in Latin America.

The gender differences of expectations also come into play for parents of trans children. In the case of transgender men, their mothers often faced hurdles to acceptance that their fathers did not face. For mothers, learning that they had a son rather than a daughter entailed letting go of the idea that their offspring would grow up to have certain shared experiences, such as motherhood. Meanwhile, transgender women often faced more rejection from their fathers than their mothers.[41]

7.2.2 Reenvisioning the Future

The two testimonies in the preceding section about motherhood highlight a fact that came up in many of our interviews: being gay did not, as many parents first thought, preclude the possibility of grandchildren. Grandparents had varying attitudes about the multiple ways in which their children became parents – including biologically through sperm donation, adoption (open, semi-open, and closed), or surrogacy. Yet, once they became grandparents, their role and love for their children – if they had accepted their children's decision – seemed to be similar to any grandparent. They picked up grandchildren at school and helped with aftercare. They took them to the doctor and on vacations. They saved the day when there were emergencies at work or school, and the grandchildren needed to be taken care of by an adult, and their parents were not available.

Once they had the opportunity to consider the possibility that they might still become grandparents, the "how" often became much less important, and the shock of reenvisioning their future family receded. Whereas a mother might have envisioned her son getting married and having biological children with his wife, a future in which he married another man and adopted children would still provide her with the opportunity to become a grandmother. And the new role as a grandparent did, in many cases, contribute to changing parents' understanding of their children (and their choices). Even parents who seem to still struggle with their children's sexual orientations and identities have no doubts about their feelings and role as grandparents. Moreover, we have observed cases in which parents had not been very accepting of their child's identity, but nevertheless, they became "terrific grandparents." Their involvement as grandparents also contributed to repairing, or in the words of one of our interviewees "patch[ing] up," their child-parent linkage.

> The truth is that they were shitty parents [...] I thought I was never going to see them again. When we had [son's name] they showed up and were

---

[41] In the case of fathers rejecting their transgender daughters, the sources of rejection were generally more related to a culture of machismo than any particular expectations about shared experiences of parenthood.

amazing. It's hard for me to understand that they were shitty parents, but they are present grandparents. I would tell you that our bond was repaired almost completely. The love they have for my children [there are two children now] is indescribable. The fact that they are such present grandparents forgives them a little for having been such awful parents.

Of course, not all same-sex couples choose to get married or have children. But for those who do, it can often contribute to tolerance and acceptance, particularly among parents who initially reacted negatively. Changes in public policy that have enabled same-sex couples to get married and adopt, as well as technologies that enable reproduction, such as IVF and surrogacy, allow same-sex couples to live lives similar to many heterosexual couples. The legal recognition of same-sex couples and their rights to adopt, and the advancement of technologies (and businesses) that enable in vitro pregnancies and the use of surrogacy, changed the landscape of how individuals and couples (heterosexual, homosexual) form families.

The role of personal experience

These new ways of building a family were less novel for those who had gone through a (traumatic) separation, as well as those living in less traditional and more modern arrangements – having children outside of marriage, raising children together with a partner who also has children from a prior relationship. Parents' personal experiences with divorce and less traditional family arrangements often contributed to their acceptance of their child's future family with a same-sex partner. Parents in these situations are more likely to have a nuanced understanding of marriage and diversity. As such, they are often more open to challenging traditional ideas about marriage and family.

See, for example, Figure 12, which presents data from LAPOP's AmericasBarometer 2023 surveys. Parents who are not currently married are significantly more likely than married parents to approve of legalizing same-sex marriage and same-sex adoptions. The "unmarried" category includes those that are divorced, separated, single, or living with a partner but not married.[42]

---

[42] We exclude widow(er)s and those in civil unions from the figure. Respondents in civil unions (comprising only 0.3 percent of parents in the sample) are the most supportive; widow(er)s (4 percent of parents) are the least supportive. We exclude widow(er)s because they are neither married nor part of a nontraditional family structure. Nonetheless, if we include widow(er)s (who are, on average, 21 years older than other parents in the sample) in the "unmarried" category, we still observe a large difference between the two groups (including widow(er)s reduces support by about one percentage point on both outcomes). Note also that we only have data on current marital status – respondents who previously experienced divorce but later married a new partner will only show up in the data as "married."

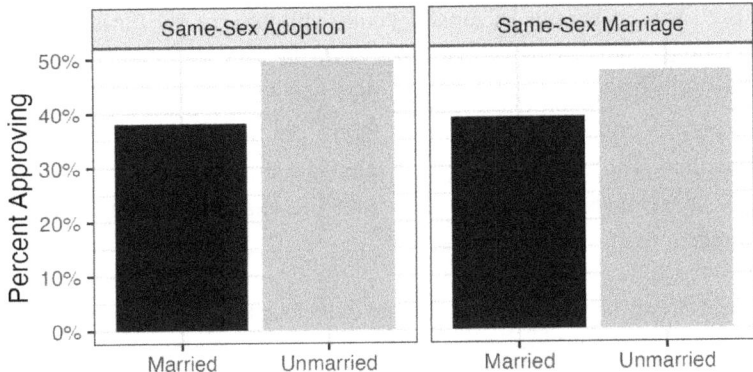

Figure 12 Support for LGBTQ+ rights among Married and unmarried parents.

Note: LAPOP 2023 data. Approval is defined as a response of greater than five on a scale of one ("completely disapprove") to ten ("completely approve"). "Married" includes all currently married parents (even those who might have divorced another partner in the past). "Unmarried" includes parents who are single, divorced, separated, or living with a partner (but not married). Countries include Argentina, Belize, Bolivia, Brazil, Chile, Costa Rica, the Dominican Republic, El Salvador, Guatemala, Mexico, Panama, Peru, and Uruguay.

These data do not establish a causal relationship – after all, marital status correlates with many other predictors of support for LGBTQ+ rights. But even when we control for religiosity, age, education, gender, and urban/rural residence, we still find that marital status is a statistically significant predictor of views on same-sex marriage and adoption.[43]

Moreover, qualitative evidence bolsters the argument that personal experience with divorce in particular can influence attitudes about LGBTQ+ families, as interviewees explained in their own words how this experience changed their mindset. The influence of demographic shifts in family formation – particularly the rise in divorce – came up frequently in interviews. In addition to generating more openness to nontraditional family structures, the experience of divorce was, for some, an initial experience with major life changes that contributed to their reaction to a loved one coming out. Individuals who experience divorce are often forced to reconsider their futures; they had imagined they would remain with this partner for the rest of their lives, and were now reenvisioning how the rest of their life would look.

---

[43] These linear regressions also include country fixed effects. The outcome variables were kept in their original format of 0–10 scales of approval. For same-sex marriage, the estimated coefficient on "unmarried" is 0.50 ($p < 0.001$) among parents and 0.92 ($p < 0.001$) among nonparents; for adoption, it is 0.59 ($p < 0.001$) among parents and 0.64 ($p < 0.05$) among nonparents. See Online Appendix for full regression results.

In the cases of parents of mostly young children (at the time of divorce), many of them have to come to terms with the fact that their children will also have a different life than the one they had envisioned. Almost everyone who separates and has children must figure out how to live a life they had not imagined. Those who successfully navigate this challenge tend to be prepared – consciously or not – to deal with life changes. As one interviewee explained:

> I had already begun to question the idea of lifelong love after my separation. We got married for life and we didn't even last seven years. It took me a lot to get used to being a divorced dad. My parents are still together and I didn't have many friends who had separated at that time... now I have a bunch of friends. Let's say we were the first... the pioneers of divorce in the group. When [son's name] told us that he was gay I was more prepared. Let me be honest, I was very shocked, well not that much because it was kind of obvious, but anyway, it's one thing to think about it and another thing to know it. Anyway, I had already lived and survived completely changing what I thought my life was going to be, and I am happy. I understood it instantly and obviously, the mother and I always supported him.

Qualitative evidence suggests that having gone through a similar experience of reenvisioning one's future after divorce left some parents more ready and able to do the same when their children came out. The testimony below, from someone who got divorced in her early thirties with a child, describes many of the feelings and reflections others shared with us. It represents how the lived experience of a sudden separation and the end of an idea of how married life was going to be, provided the interviewee with "lightness" and wisdom to navigate her son's coming out as a young teenager:

> Once you split up, once you go through that drama and survive, you gain lightness. I would say maturity. It took me years, more than a decade, to really recover. Rebuild myself, understand the failure of my marriage. It was very hard [...] In addition, it caught me off guard; I didn't see it coming [...] Once you go through that, you have more lightness and more flexibility to understand that life gives you surprises. More importantly, I knew everything was going to be okay because I already went through it once. Furthermore, now I am older, I have more maturity and more life lived.

Indeed, we do not expect this experience to be universal, as many individuals who have experienced life-changing events might seek stability and dislike any changes in their expectations. Still, the evidence indicates that those who have lived through divorce and separations often tended to have an easier time accepting their loved ones' sexual orientations and identities.

8 Public Policy and LGBTQ+ Rights

We began this Element with the observation that public opinion has shifted dramatically in recent decades in Latin America (and, indeed, across much of the world). At the same time, the public policy landscape has also shifted, with LGBTQ+ communities winning legal battles for basic rights and equality under the law.

To provide an account of attitude change in Latin America without addressing the role of public policy would be to neglect an essential part of the story. From the AIDS crisis, to same-sex marriage and adoption rights, to gender identity laws, public policy has been intimately related to the trajectory of LGBTQ+ acceptance.

8.1 Public Opinion: Leading or Following Public Policy?

Scholars have long noted the close relationship between public opinion and public policy. Flores and Barclay (2016) propose four distinct ways that public opinion might relate to public policy: backlash, legitimacy, polarization, and consensus. The first three are models by which public policy shapes public opinion: advances in LGBTQ+ rights could spark a *backlash*, generating more negative attitudes towards LGBTQ+ people; it could lend greater *legitimacy* to LGB relationships and LGBTQ+ identities, generating more tolerance and acceptance; or it could cause *polarization*, where people are less likely to say that they have no opinion and both positive and negative attitudes become stronger. The *consensus* model, by contrast, proposes that public opinion drives public policy – and public policy changes do not then shape public opinion.

Recent studies have found compelling evidence that codifying LGBTQ+ rights contributes to further acceptance. Aksoy et al. (2020) use a difference-in-differences design to analyze the effect of expanding same-sex relationship recognition policies (same-sex marriage, but also domestic partnerships) on attitudes toward gay and lesbian people in Europe. Drawing on public opinion data from the European Social Survey, they analyze over 325,000 responses to a question asking whether "Gay men and lesbians should be free to live their own life as they wish." They find compelling evidence that expanding same-sex relationship recognition policies leads to greater tolerance. The effect is consistent, with not a single case of policy causing any backlash, and substantively large. Over the 14-year period they study, agreement with the statement that "gay men and lesbians should be free to live their own life as they wish" increased by ten percentage points. The authors are able to attribute 35 percent of this positive shift to the effect of public policy changes. They bolster their evidence of a causal story by showing that these public policy changes do not bear any systematic relationship with attitudes on other social and economic issues, such as attitudes towards immigrants. In another study, Kenny and Patel (2017) employ a similar design to probe the effects of legalizing homosexuality in countries around the world. They too find that expanding rights generated increased tolerance toward LGBTQ+ individuals.

But not every study paints such a positive picture. Studies of the US public's response to the legalization of same-sex marriage have mixed findings. Recent studies cast doubt on the backlash hypothesis (Bishin et al. 2016) and find that same-sex marriage legalization can improve attitudes when passed by state legislatures (Ofosu et al. 2019). But when studying the impact of the US Supreme Court ruling in favor of same-sex marriage (*Obergefell v. Hodges*), other studies fail to find positive effects on attitudes towards gay and lesbian people (Tankard & Paluck 2017), or find evidence that marriage equality can indeed generate backlash when it is enacted through the courts (Ofosu et al. 2019).

A recent study of public opinion and LGBTQ+ rights in Latin America found evidence for none of the relationships that Flores and Barclay propose. De Abreu Maia et al. (2023) constructed the Latin American Rainbow Index (LARI), a measure of LGBTQ+ rights that incorporates a variety of policies including same-sex marriage, adoption, the right to serve openly in the military, nondiscrimination protections, and legal recognition of gender identity. Combining their new measure with LAPOP survey data, they look for evidence that changes in a country's LARI score affected public opinion. They do not find evidence that policy changes improved public opinion, sparked a backlash, or polarized opinions. Moreover, when they look at the other direction of causality – did public opinion lead to policy change? – they also find no statistical relationship.

De Abreu Maia et al.'s results are surprising. In most other world regions, scholars have found evidence of some type of relationship between LGBTQ+ rights and public opinion. In our interviews with activists, many stressed the importance of changing people's minds (*ganar la calle*) to achieve effective change. And in our conversations of LGBTQ+ individuals and their families, we saw examples of how policy change made acceptance more likely. Recall the discussion in Section 7 of how many parents became more accepting of their gay and lesbian children upon learning that they still intended to get married and start a family – a possibility that came after years of fighting for gay and lesbian couples' right to marry. More broadly, extending rights to a minority group allows its members to participate more fully in society – a key step in facilitating acceptance.

But there are reasons why these relationships might not show up in the statistical analysis. Regarding the influence of public policy on public opinion, the effects we observe are not direct effects as theorized by Flores and Barclay, where the mere act of passing a law confers legitimacy and changes public opinion. Instead, it is a gradual process by which these new laws change the lives that LGBTQ+ people can live. And on the extent to which public opinion makes public policy change feasible, the paths to legal victory for LGBTQ+ advocates have varied widely across cases in the region. Some victories came in the legislature; many others came through the courts, which are less constrained by public opinion.

In this section, we discuss some of the key tools that activists can use to achieve policy change. Finally, we draw on three cases – Argentina, Brazil, and Bolivia – to illustrate how the set of tools that activists used in specific cases shaped both policy outcomes and attitudes.

8.2 Paths to Victory: The Activist's Toolbox

Activists seeking policy change have many different tools at their disposal. Here, we discuss four key dimensions of activist strategies for policy change: the venue for legal change (new legislation versus court rulings); involvement with political parties; the framing of LGBTQ+ rights; and international pressures.

8.2.1 Congress or the Courts?

Policy change can come from new laws, or from new interpretations of existing laws. Often, activists have pushed to reinterpret existing laws via appeals to judges. Indeed, most Latin American countries that have established the right of same-sex marriage did so through the courts. Of the eight countries that have achieved marriage equality, only three (all in the Southern Cone) passed same-sex marriage legislation through Congress: Argentina (2010), Uruguay (2013), and Chile (2022). The remaining five countries achieved achieved marriage equality via court rulings.

Working through the courts is sometimes the fastest route to policy change. When appealing to judges, activists can achieve change without waiting for mass public opinion shifts. But this pathway also has shortcomings. Rights that are established without broad support may not be protected as well in practice. Citizens might not attribute the same legitimacy to a right established by a reinterpretation of the law, compared to a right established by new legislation.

And policy changes that occur without broad support are more likely to face obstacles in implementation. Bureaucrats, for example, might abuse their discretion as a means of resisting the new policy. One particularly well-publicized example comes from the United States, where a Kentucky county clerk refused to issue marriage certificates for gay couples, in defiance of the U.S. Supreme Court ruling legalizing same-sex marriage nationwide (as well as a subsequent U.S. District Court order). In many locales, transgender individuals seeking legal name or gender changes can face hostility depending on which judge or bureaucrat is tasked with processing their request.

These limits of advancing progress through the courts can be seen in a variety of policy contexts. To take another issue as an example, Daby and Moseley (2024) show how this argument played out in the context of abortion decriminalization and legalization in Latin America. Congressional decisions to honor doctors and nurses who invoke their rights to conscientious objection to the practice of abortion has effectively led to the absence of abortion provision in rural and conservative areas of countries where abortion is legal (Casas 2009; Küng et al. 2021; Undurraga & Sadler 2019). Daby and Moseley (2024) highlight the importance of maintaining constant and systematic support from feminist movements on the streets to ensure that judicial rulings effectively change people's lives.

Court rulings are often an effective way to achieve legal victories that aren't yet possible through the legislature. But a lack of "mass-based activism and effective public outreach strategies" truncates the "rights-affirming promise of judicialization" (Botero 2022: 23).

The question of whether to pursue change via congress or the courts is not necessarily an "either/or" dilemma for activists: often, they simultaneously pursue both paths. Within marriage equality movements, activists with legal backgrounds and contacts in the judicial system work to build legal cases for sympathetic judges. Meanwhile, activists more familiar with legislation work with politicians and allies in each party to build coalitions to support a same-sex marriage bill.

8.2.2 Political Parties

Another key decision activists face is how to approach political parties. Building alliances with major political parties holds some appeal. The parties have agenda-setting power: building close ties to the ruling party is one way that activists can get their priorities on the legislative agenda. Parties are also key actors in the design and implementation of public policy. Given their central role in decision making and implementation of policies that are central to LGBTQ+ actors, the need for relationships that enable the exchange of ideas, information and feedback is critical to the success of building and passing new legislation.

Parties also shape public opinion. Citizens who identify with a political party often react to leaders' cues about policy preferences, and shift some of their own preferences to align with the party's platform. And parties have access to immense resources that could be marshalled to promote an aligned activist group's political goals.

But alliances with political parties have proved risky for LGBTQ+ activists. Although parties can shift public opinion on many issues, their supporters will not blindly follow any elite cue. Parties have greater ability to shift public opinion on issues where citizens do not already hold particularly strong opinions – such as on the details of a public policy or other technocratic matters. But it is much more difficult to shift supporters' fundamental values – or their positions on issues that they see as inextricably linked to those values. If public opinion turns against a pro-LGBTQ+ policy, parties might abandon the issue rather than risk their electoral future.

Even durable alliances between parties and activists pose some risks. When voters begin to associate a policy position with a particular party, the issue itself can transform into a partisan matter. There is nothing inherently partisan about same-sex marriage; but if voters view the issue as a particular party's issue, it becomes vulnerable to partisan divisions. When activists work independently from parties, they might be able to reach broad consensus over time; but by linking the issue to divisive parties, they can create a lower ceiling on potential public support.

The same logic can apply to specific government programs. After Javier Milei was elected, his administration closed the Ministry of Women, Gender, and Diversity created in 2019. In a viral video, when he was a candidate for the presidency, Milei stepped up on a blackboard with the names of Ministries and Secretaries of the state and screamed out "Ministry of Women, Gender, and Diversity." As soon as he became President, he converted the Ministry into a secretary to close it six months later. In an official statement, the Minister of Justice of his government stated that "this organization was created and used by the previous administration for political-partisan purposes to propagate and impose an ideological agenda, hire activists, and organize talks and events." Diana Mondino, Argentina's councilor, wrote on X "Say goodbye to the Ministry of Women and Sandwiches that has left."

The decision to shut down the Ministry was part of a broader agenda of opposing anything the administration defines as "gender ideology." Yet the Ministry of Women, Gender, and Diversity was seen by many in the population – including many feminist activists – as a partisan institution that did little for poor women and those suffering domestic violence. The Ministry's main activities were to organize workshops which did little to improve the lives of those suffering discrimination and violence. Given that most of the Ministry's budget was spent on paying salaries of public employees who, in most cases, supported the previous Peronist administration, it was hard to defend their work as independent and effective – regardless of whether it was. This case illustrates the risks that activists and policy-makers run when they tie a political issue to a particular political party. In this case, the more that their solutions to the issue of violence against women were seen as *Peronist* solutions, the more vulnerable they became to public opinion turning against them once there was a change of government.

8.2.3 LGBTQ+ Rights as Human Rights

One way that activists can work towards consensus is by reframing a controversial issue within a framework of values that people already hold. In Latin America, some of the most successful efforts to achieve broad acceptance of LGBTQ+ rights were those in which activists made a strategic decision to frame LGBTQ+ rights as *human* rights, rather than civil rights. Encarnación (2018) points to a distinction between civil rights appeals as focusing on legislation to achieve specific rights within a country's legal framework, versus human rights appeals focusing on concepts such as "freedom of sexuality." A human rights appeal implies certain legislation and policies; but these legislative implications are downstream from a moral appeal. A human rights framing appeals to a universality (*all* people should have freedom of sexuality) rather than a fundamentally group-based appeal (sexual minorities should have certain legal protections). And in Latin America, the discourse of human rights holds historical importance that shapes its effectiveness.

Latin American countries experienced transitions to democracy and the market in the 1980s and 1990s (O'Donnell & Schmitter 1986; Przeworski 1991). In countries where transitional justice was attained, human rights organizations played a crucial role in achieving justice for human rights violations, including the disappearance of people (Gonzalez-Ocantos 2019; Sikkink 2011). Building on the influence and success of human rights organizations, movements that deployed a human rights framework were more effective in enfranchising LGBTQ+ people than movements that framed enfranchisement as a political struggle for civil rights. Latin America's LGBTQ+ activists' decision to pursue equality for their community as a human-rights concern rather than a specific legal issue was a savvy strategy that resonated with societies that have experienced gruesome human rights violations (Encarnación 2016).

Winning the support of human rights organizations was crucial to increasing support for gay and lesbian organizations. Human rights organizations in

Latin America count on broad support and legitimacy among citizens These organizations were mostly focused on recovering the identities and bodies of the disappeared and bringing to justice those in charge of committing torture, rape, assassinations, and child appropriation. Initially, human rights were never associated with sexuality. Even references to sexual violence during tortures and disappearance were only more recently explored (Lewin & Wornat 2020). But gay activists connected their struggle with human rights activists, stating that freedom of sexuality was a fundamental human right (Encarnación 2018: 198).

Initially, many human rights activists did not share gay activists' understanding of sexual rights as human rights. Many of them "saw gay activists 'as extra-terrestrial' and regarded working with gay issues 'detrimental to their own cause.'" (Interview with Mabel Bellucci by Encarnación 2018: 202). But some gay activists persisted, and they were able to build alliances with human rights organizations after establishing close relationships with the organizations' leadership. Gay rights organizations that sought out alliances with human rights organizations were not only seeking their endorsement; they also sought to build upon many of the strategies that human rights organizations had used, such as targeting public opinion, shaming public officials, and building international connections with other organizations abroad (Keck & Sikkink 1998).

8.2.4 International Pressures

International forces play an important role in shaping the trajectory of public policy change. A clear example of this was the involvement of ACT UP activists in the US when Argentine President Carlos Menem visited Columbia University's School of Public and International Affairs to speak in November 1991. Menem was on a tour of the US, aiming to sell a renewed image of Argentina and tout its economic and political development as a modern democracy.

But during his visit, Menem faced scrutiny over Argentina's refusal to grant legal status to the CHA (*Comunidad Homosexual Argentina*), an association formed in 1984 to fight for LGBTQ+ rights. Months before Menem's visit, the Argentine Supreme Court denied the CHA's proposal to receive NGO status (*personería jurídica*). The court justified its ruling, arguing that the CHA did not fulfill the objective of providing services for the good of the community (*bien común*).

Columbia held a Q&A following Menem's speech. During the Q&A, one of the ACT UP activists questioned how democratic Argentina really was if it was denying the CHA the right to free association. Menem had faced public pressure in the US on this issue for some time, and he was unsurprised by the question (Bazán 2006: 374). In response, he stated that he had already issued instructions to reverse the court's decision. As one activist who was present that day noted, "The Argentine press corps took frantic notes, talked into their tape recorders, and hurriedly made long-distance calls. They were as surprised as we were" (González 2008). The events at Columbia made headlines in Argentina; and a few months later, in March 1992, CHA gained legal status via a decree from Menem, reversing the court's decision.

Another example of the role that international pressures can play comes from Costa Rica. In 2016, Costa Rica requested an interpretation of the right to privacy and equal protection under the American Convention on Human Rights from the Inter-American Court of Human Rights (IACHR). In 2017, the Inter-American Court of Human Rights issued a landmark opinion stating that all rights applicable to heterosexual couples should extend to same-sex couples. One year later (in 2018), the Costa Rican Supreme Court ruled in favor of marriage equality, citing the Inter-American Court's opinion. The court gave the Legislative Assembly 18 months to reform the law, or the ban would be lifted automatically. In 2020, with no legislative action taken, the ban on same-sex marriage was automatically lifted on May 26, 2020, making Costa Rica the first country in Central America to legalize same-sex marriage.

But elsewhere in Central America, the IACHR did not have the same influence. A key takeaway is that international forces can provide momentum, sometimes serving as the final push to a legal victory. But there must be preexisting organizational support within the country for anything to happen. These efforts did not originate abroad; rather, they started at home, and local activists leveraged international pressures to help the process along.

***

Turning to case studies, we can see these different strategies in action. In Argentina, changing public opinion was central to the fight for same-sex marriage. In Brazil, activists achieved marriage equality through the courts after partisan alliances failed. And in Bolivia, where public opinion lags far behind legal progress on trans rights, we find an example of how legal successes can be blunted by weaker progress on public opinion. We use these case studies to illustrate the effects of different strategies, and the diverse paths that activists have taken to achieve progress. These cases are not counterfactuals to one another – in each country, activists face different structural constraints and political dynamics. However, beyond their contextual and structural differences, they illustrate the importance of building resonant framing and strategic alliances to achieve changes in attitudes.

8.3 *Ganar la calle*: Same-sex Marriage in Argentina

"These issues that have to do with the human condition, these things that have to do with the aspiration for equality that every society should have, are things that cannot divide us; they are things that, to the contrary, should unite us. Today we are a society that is a little more egalitarian than the one we were last week."

These were the words of Argentina's then-president Cristina Fernández de Kirchner when she signed into law a 2010 bill legalizing same-sex marriage in Argentina – making Argentina the first in Latin America, the second in the Americas (after Canada), and the tenth in the world to legalize same-sex marriage. In the same speech, she evoked the image of Eva Perón advancing women's right to vote 58 years prior.

Upon signing the same-sex marriage bill into law, President Cristina Fernández de Kirchner observed just how much had changed in the country to lead to that moment. She noted, "If this had been proposed years ago, it would have been impossible." How did same-sex marriage move from an impossibility to the law of the land?

8.3.1 "Show Me the Polls"

Public opinion was crucial to the fight for marriage equality in Argentina. Activists described politicians as addicted to polls, so they tried to use the polls to convince them that the bill had public support. In a 2007 meeting, then-Minister of Interior Aníbal Fernández informed activists that on a personal level, he supported the measure. As a private individual, he did not need convincing; but as Minister – in his public position – he needed more if he was going to push his government to support a bill:

> Guys, I already told you that I am already convinced. I totally agree with you. Now, I'm not going to lie to you, I can't make a commitment today. That does not mean that the Government is not going to support the marriage law, but it is a scenario that must be built. Let's work together. You have to create conditions in which the Government feels that it can move forward with this issue and win the fight. Count on me for that. (Dialogue between the Federación and the Minister of Interior, Aníbal Fernández 3 August 2007 quoted in Bimbi 2011: 89.)

Creating the conditions in which politicians would openly support the same-sex marriage bill implied winning the streets – and changing the polls. Activists used the politics of respectability to advance their ideas. Insisting that love is love, they constantly repeated that the opinion of others – those who rejected same-sex marriage – must not prevent people who were in love from marrying each other. They began sharing stories that illustrated the real-life consequences that the lack of legal recognition had for gay and lesbian couples. They spoke about cases where someone's partner died, but the surviving partner was not able to inherit their late partner's property or receive a pension. Stories of parents who had rejected their children for being gay, but later had no problem inheriting their wealth or property, did not sit well with the public. Even among people who were uncomfortable with homosexuality, many concurred that partners who had lived together and built a life together should be entitled to inheritance and pensions just as much as heterosexual couples.

Activists repeatedly spoke about scenarios in which same-sex couples suffered because they lacked the rights that married couples had (e.g., making medical decisions, inheriting pensions and properties). This strategy worked to raise consciousness about the injustice. By shifting the conversation to the actual benefits of marriage, they amassed greater support. Activists also worked tirelessly to change the meaning of marriage. When they succeeded in defining marriage as a union of two people who love each other, the case against same-sex marriage was hard to defend.

In pushing for same-sex marriage rather than civil unions, Argentine activists drew on lessons from Spain. In conversations with Argentine activists, Pedro Zerolo, a Spanish former politician and a key advocate for same-sex marriage in his country, insisted that Argentine activists should ask for marriage as they did in Spain:

> Asking for civil union means resigning yourself to accepting second-class rights for second-class citizens. We are not fighting for inheritance or pensions, we are fighting for our dignity and legal equality, which can only be achieved through marriage. Furthermore, as long as we talk about civil unions, we will be told no. When we start talking about marriage, we will be offered civil unions. And that is where they lose because they are exposed: if they accept that our families must be recognized, why create a new institution with another name? What is the point? It is there where it becomes clear that the foundation for their argument is discrimination. And we won that debate. (Zerolo in conversation with Argentine activists. Quoted in Bimbi 2011: 25.)

Activists' success in changing opinions could be seen in the polls. However, when activists began showing sympathetic but skeptical politicians that the polls were now on their side, politicians responded that their polls were not representative of the whole country. They insisted that those numbers only reflected the metropolitan areas of the country and in "the rest of the country they lose by a large margin (*por afano*), the Church weighs more and society is more conservative" (Bimbi 2011: 128).

Activist organizations began conducting focus groups and observed how participants expressed accepting views towards LGBTQ+ people and same-sex marriage. They again found that the majority of people supported same-sex marriage; many even thought (mistakenly) that same-sex marriage was already legal. One young participant in the focus groups summed up the change from rejection to tolerance, saying "What's the problem if you are gay? We need to live and let live" (Bimbi 2011: 131).

In 2008, LGBTQ+ organizations conducted a national poll and found that 66 percent of Argentines supported same-sex marriage (Bimbi 2011). When the same-sex bill became law, many citizens, especially the youngest ones, fully supported these changes.

8.3.2 After Legalization

The bill passed with plenty of opposition – 126 deputies in the Argentine Congress voted in favor, while 110 voted against it; in the Senate, the vote was 33 to 27. And yet, Fernández de Kirchner anticipated that support would only continue to grow, predicting that "in a few years, this will turn out to be an absolutely anachronistic debate."

Indeed, in the decade and a half since Argentina legalized same-sex marriage, support for the institution has continued to rise. In 2010, 60 percent of Argentines supported the institution;[44] today, 72 percent support it.[45]

Of course, mass public opinion shift does not occur in a vacuum. Major public opinion leaders – including political and religious figures – changed their tone on same-sex marriage over time. One of the most notable shifts came from Pope Francis. In 2010, then-Archbishop of Buenos Aires, Jorge Mario Bergoglio, campaigned against the same-sex marriage bill. At the time, he stated that same-sex marriage was the devil's "attempt to destroy God's plan." He further claimed that the fight for marriage equality was "not a simple political struggle; it is a destructive attempt at God's plan. This is not a mere legislative project (this is only the instrument) but a 'move' by the father of lies that seeks to confuse and deceive the children of God" (Encarnación 2018, p. 205).

But after he assumed the papacy, his tone changed dramatically. Early on, he made headlines for responding to a question by saying "If someone is gay and seeks the Lord with good will, who am I to judge?" Preaching publicly about a recurrent episode in confessionals where parents ask for advice about how to deal with a gay child, the Pope asked parents not to condemn their

---

[44] LAPOP 2010 survey.
[45] LAPOP 2023 survey.

children for their sexual orientation: "Homosexuals have a right to be accepted by their families as children and siblings." Pope Francis walked a fine line on LGBTQ+ issues, maintaining a complicated position – and often a seemingly contradictory one. He often preached tolerance toward LGBTQ+ individuals; yet he continued to make public statements about the supposed negative societal implications of LGBTQ+ identities (hence his overarching message falls far short of complete acceptance). The Pope regularly welcomed a group of transgender sex workers into the Vatican, providing them with food and other forms of assistance (Winfield & Thomas 2023). And he recently approved an official Church statement, inviting transgender people to be baptized and serve as godparents (Knox 2023). But in 2015, he "condemn[ed] 'gender theory,' comparing it to nuclear war and genetic manipulation" (Fullam 2015). And he maintained the view later that "gender ideology" is an "ugly ideology" (Reuters 2024). Nonetheless, his papacy was far more tolerant toward LGBTQ+ people than that of his predecessors. Religion scholars, biographers, and close friends of the late Pope have speculated about the extent to which Pope Francis's private beliefs changed. Yet putting aside the issue of how his personal beliefs shifted, the shift in his *public* statements signaled the changing environment for attitudes toward LGBTQ+ communities. Moreover, such a shift from the head of the Catholic Church can also create a permission structure for religious individuals to embrace a more tolerant – or even accepting – mindset without abandoning their identity as Catholics. As the head of the Catholic Church, of course, Pope Francis was not merely an opinion leader in Argentina. But his position as the first Pope from Argentina (and from Latin America) lends particular significance to his statements in Argentina, where they frequently received extensive media coverage and were interpreted in terms of domestic political dynamics.

President Cristina Fernández de Kirchner also changed her tone over time on same-sex marriage. Her public support for same-sex marriage came only after the polls had started to move in favor of it. But more recently, President Kirchner herself recalls in her biography that, referring to LGBTQ+ rights, she "do[es] not like the word 'tolerance'," as she see the term as implying that "I 'have to put up with' those who are different from me because I have no other choice, and that's why I've always preferred to talk about equality." (Fernández de Kirchner 2019: 275). She also remembers how, in looking through the list of senators who supported the bill, she saw the name of a legislator who was against it and ended up voting in favor after his divorce and another one who identified as Catholic and changed his mind after listening to the testimonies from gay couples in Congress. Reflecting about her position and those of her peers, she writes, "Well... life changes us because reality changes too" (Fernández de Kirchner 2019: 216).

8.4 An "Inconvenient" Alliance: The PT in Brazil

In many ways, Brazil was a more likely case than Argentina to advance LGBTQ+ rights and legalize same-sex marriage earlier than its neighbors. The LGBTQ+ community in Brazil was larger and more organized than those in other Southern Cone countries. But activists in Brazil took a very different tack than those in Argentina. Instead of framing the fight around human rights, they relied on discourses of civil rights. And whereas the activists in Argentina maintained a safe distance from the political parties they courted, Brazilian activists built a close alliance with one political party, which impeded their ability to build a broad political coalition (Encarnación 2018).

In an effort to build political support and advance their rights, LGBTQ+ activists forged a close alliance with the *Partido dos Trabalhadores* (Worker's Party or PT). At the time, the PT was a socialist party and its Leftist ideology identified it closely with gender and sexual equality. Yet, as the party transformed from an outsider socialist party into an insider social-democratic party (Samuels 2004), the alliance proved problematic for a party interested in growing the size of their constituency. As the PT became a national party with presidential ambitions, its partnership with the gay community became "inconvenient," as anthropologist Peter Fry aptly described it. The party would not win conservative and centrist votes by vocally advocating for gay rights. Meanwhile, the party knew that even if it backed off of gay rights, it didn't run much risk of losing LGBTQ+ voters; their alternative, voting for conservative parties that opposed gay rights, would hardly be better. Thus, when the PT became a catch-all-party seeking the presidency, PT presidential candidate Lula moderated his alliance with LGBTQ+ activists and communities.

During Lula's first presidency in 2003, the President did not advance the agenda of LGBTQ+ rights. When his reelection was on the table, he even openly courted and made alliances with Evangelical pastors and politicians who were openly against LGBTQ+ rights, in an effort to win Evangelical votes. Amid the rise of socially conservative Evangelical voters who perceived an increasingly secular and progressive society as threatening to their traditional way of life, politicians were further constrained in the positions they took on LGBTQ+ rights and less willing to make alliances with LGBTQ+ activists (Boas 2020; Smith & Boas 2023).

The tone of political discussion around LGBTQ+ rights in Brazil has hardly improved in recent years. Jair Bolsonaro, elected to the presidency in 2018, openly stated that he would be "incapable of loving a gay son" and would prefer his son die in an accident rather than be gay.

He reduced government support for LGBTQ+ rights and undermined existing protections for LGBTQ+ individuals. Bolsonaro's anti-LGBTQ+ rhetoric created a climate that some LGBTQ+ activists argued emboldened homophobic violence. The president appointed Damares Alves, a conservative evangelical pastor, as the Minister of Women, Family, and Human Rights. Alves made it clear that the ministry's priorities would be aligned with conservative, Christian values, often sidelining LGBTQ+ issues. The government actively opposed the inclusion of gender and sexuality education in schools, referring to such education as "gender ideology." The president vetoed funding for LGBTQ+ film festivals and other cultural events, framing them as inappropriate uses of public money.

Despite Bolsonaro's opposition, Brazil's Supreme Court played a significant role in maintaining protections for LGBTQ+ people during his tenure. In 2019, the Court criminalized homophobia and transphobia, equating them to racial discrimination. Bolsonaro publicly criticized the decision, but it remains in effect.

Brazil did not legalize same-sex marriage as early as Argentina, but in 2013, marriage equality was won through the courts. Brazil has made substantial progress in legally recognizing LGBTQ+ rights – as of 2020, it was tied for the most legally progressive country in Latin America (de Abreu Maia et al. 2023). But this legal progress has not translated to a broad consensus in public opinion. Activists were successful in working through the courts to secure formal rights. But by working through the courts rather than public opinion, and relying on a civil rights framing, activists in Brazil were less effective in changing broader attitudes among the public.

That's not to say that attitudes haven't changed at all in Brazil. Indeed, when Lula returned to power for a third term in office (in 2023) he publicly stated his support for LGBTQ+ rights. He stated that, under his presidency, "Brazil will no longer be a country of hate, intolerance, and violence against LGBTQ+ people. We will restore dignity and respect to everyone, regardless of who they love."

And public opinion on LGBTQ+ issues has trended more positive in recent decades in Brazil – but the shift has not been nearly as dramatic as in Argentina, where activists maintained distance from political parties and campaigned on a human rights message. Between 1991 and 2018 in Brazil, positive responses to the World Values Survey's basic tolerance question ("can homosexuality be justified?") grew by 28 percentage points, from 11 to 39 percent. In Argentina, positive responses grew by *40 percentage points* over the same period, from 19 percent to 59 percent.

Other Southern Cone countries also outpaced Brazil on this measure. Support in Chile grew from 5 percent to 44 percent (39 points) from 1990 to 2018. And Uruguayans' support increased by 30 percentage points (28 percent to 58 percent) over an even shorter time span (data from Uruguay are only available for the 15-year period of 1996–2011, as opposed to the 27-year period observed in Brazil).

Activists elsewhere saw great success in allying with human rights organizations – organizations that relied upon a sense of legitimacy across a broad majority of society, enabling them to work with different administrations. The perceived lack of partisanship in their demands enabled citizens with different political affiliations to participate in these organizations. In contrast, when LGBTQ+ rights are seen as partisan rather than universal issues, cultural battles emerge and partisan divisions can prevent consensus.

8.5 De Jure versus De Facto: Trans Rights in Bolivia

Bolivia is, in many ways, a puzzling case. The LARI index ranks it as the fifth strongest country on LGBTQ+ rights in 2020 – ahead of countries including Mexico and Chile (de Abreu Maia et al. 2023). It was one of the first countries to allow transgender individuals to legally change their gender without surgical requirements. And the country broadly prohibits discrimination on the basis of sexual orientation and gender identity.

Yet public opinion on LGBTQ+ issues is hardly positive in Bolivia. Recall Figures 4 and 5 from Section 2, illustrating support for equal rights for LGB and trans individuals across 13 Latin American countries. Bolivia ranked third from the bottom on support for LGB rights and fifth from the bottom on trans rights. Only 40 percent of Bolivians support same-sex marriage, compared to 74 percent in Chile, 69 percent in Mexico, and 53 percent in Peru – all countries that rank below Bolivia on the LARI index.

And the lived experience of LGBTQ+ individuals in Bolivia lags behind countries that score lower on the LARI index. Whereas 68 percent of Chileans and 69 percent of Mexicans describe their home as a "good place for for gay and lesbian people to live," just 40 percent of Bolivians do – putting it ahead of only Paraguay, Guatemala, and the Dominican Republic. (Bolivia is tied with Peru on this metric.)

In Bolivia, trans activists succeeded in pushing the government to add an anti-discrimination clause in the 2009 Bolivian Constitution and pass a national gender identity law. The majority of the voters of the country did not support these changes; yet activists' strong ties to the government enabled them to lobby for these changes despite the lack of public support and the open rejection from conservative groups. Explaining activists' success, Hummel and Velasco-Guachalla (2024: 322) highlight how "trans activists in Bolivia leveraged their increased access to legislators in the Movement Towards Socialism (MAS) party and benefited from the expansion of LGBTQ+ legislation across the region."

On paper, trans individuals in Bolivia have access to more protections than trans individuals in some states in the United States. But in practice, the everyday life of a trans person in Bolivia is not safer than one living in the United States. Establishing formal rights is an essential step to securing equal rights in practice; but when rights are formally established without public support, they remain vulnerable.

The relentless work of Bolivian activists achieved significant legal changes that did not immediately translate into increasing tolerance and acceptance from the population. Hence, in spite of a nondiscrimination clause in the constitution, everyday discrimination is common. Moreover, when people perceive that the government has instituted a major change – in this case, the extension of trans rights – without the support of the people the government is tasked with representing, it is easy for opposition groups to challenge the law's legitimacy.

In the case of Bolivia, the fact that trans rights were so intertwined with a political party and lacked broad support from society, makes these rights – even if they are included in a constitutional clause – fragile in a region where constitutional change is common (Negretto 2013). Studying the legalization of abortion in neighboring Peru, Daby and Moseley (2024) offered a cautionary story about extending legal rights without public support: "One of the lessons of the Peruvian case is that progressive court victories could have limited effects and even unleash a solid conservative reaction when they do not count on civil society's support" (68). Recent studies do not find evidence of a backlash effect from LGBTQ+ rights legalization in Latin America (de Abreu Maia et al. 2023). Yet the case of Bolivia does make clear the limitations of working closely with a political party to achieve legal recognition without an effective public opinion campaign. Even when such a strategy yields legal victories, the impact of those victories on people's lives is blunted by a lack of public support.

***

The cases we have described here are not pure counterfactuals, where one set of activists made the "right" decisions and others made the "wrong" decisions.

Yet the differing paths activists took help to illustrate the comparative potential and limitations of alternative strategies. Looking beyond these three countries, achieving progress is not as simple as mimicking the behavior of activists who were successful elsewhere. Activists do not merely choose from a menu of strategies, static across time, place, and issue topic. Indeed, the macropolitical and organizational factors that shape which strategies are available to LGBTQ+ activists in different contexts is a major question that warrants further study in future research. What we can say here is: when activists are able to achieve policy wins through legislative action and changing public opinion; when they are able to do so without becoming inextricably tied to one political party; when they manage to connect LGBTQ+ rights to broadly held values such as human rights; and when they leverage international pressures to force domestic entities to act, they are likely to achieve broader and more enduring progress.

9 Conclusions

Across Latin America, recent decades have brought a trend toward greater tolerance and acceptance of LGBTQ+ communities. Younger generations have grown up in a world where LGBTQ+ identities are more widely acknowledged and respected. Many of them have known an openly gay person since childhood; they might even have friends with gay parents. Not all young people support LGBTQ+ rights, of course; but for many, other people's sexuality and gender identity are a nonissue.

But the change in attitudes is not just driven by young people who have grown up with accepting attitudes. We also observe many instances of individual-level change over time – from the conservative parent of a child who came out as gay, to a working-class waiter at a restaurant frequented by gay tourists, we see how personal interactions with LGBTQ+ people challenge negative stereotypes and push people to reconsider what someone's sexuality means about them as a person.

These changes rarely happen overnight; usually, it is a slow and gradual process. Not everyone changes their mind following positive interactions with LGBTQ+ individuals. And some people move toward acceptance, but then return to intolerant views as LGBTQ+ issues get politicized. But for all the progress that remains to be made on achieving broad acceptance of LGBTQ+ individuals, people around the region have come a long way in just the last few decades.

Further contributing to the transformation of public opinion, we have seen more positive representations in media and popular culture; the rise of a more expansive conception of what a family looks like; and the efforts of activists to win public support by framing LGBTQ+ rights as human rights.

Some aspects of the story of progress we have chronicled are specific to the countries we study here. Explanations emerging from the precise historical path of one country cannot be simply picked up and dropped onto another country. Yet for all the historical specificity of factors such as the economic shifts that brought hospitality workers into contact with gay customers, or the widespread public commitment to human rights after authoritarian experiences, the underlying mechanisms point to more general human tendencies. When people get to know outgroup members or learn about their stories in a way that humanizes them and fosters empathy, they often become more tolerant and accepting. In the case of LGBTQ+ acceptance, the dynamics are somewhat unique. Often people know someone LGBTQ+ before they know that person is LGBTQ+. Whereas people might choose to wall themselves off from an outgroup that they dislike, limiting the chances for empathy-fostering interactions, it becomes much harder to do this when a loved one reveals that they are actually a member of that outgroup – long after one has already developed a personal and emotional connection to this person.

These questions of generalizability point to avenues for future research. Thinking of the transformation we saw among waiters in Buenos Aires, have similar processes unfolded in other cities around the world that became major destinations for gay tourism? In countries where attitudes toward LGBTQ+ individuals have plateaued or even started to turn more negative, could some of the successes that activists have achieved in Latin America serve as a blueprint? Should we expect the acceptance of trans people in the coming decades to look more similar to the current level of acceptance of LGB people? We have touched on attitudes toward trans people, but our data on the trans experience is comparatively limited. Additional focused analysis of trans issues will help to crystallize both the similarities and differences between the trajectory of trans acceptance vs LGB acceptance. Is trans acceptance following the same path, just at a later point in time? Or will the path be fundamentally different, owing to factors such as the smaller number of trans people, the fact that many trans people choose to keep their identity and history private, or the medical aspects of surgeries and hormone treatments that are essential to many trans people's lives?

9.1 Looking Forward: Continued Progress or Risk of Moving Backwards?

The story emerging out of Latin America is one of incredible progress. Yet progress can be undone. Turning to another continent, in another century, the sobering history of 20th century Germany highlights that the fight for progress never ends and must be continually defended. In the early 20th century, Germany was home to a "flourishing gay and lesbian culture" (Heger 1994: 9). In 1919, Magnus Hirschfeld founded the Institute for Sexual Research (*Institut für Sexualwissenschaft*), a pioneering research institute and medical practice that performed some of the earliest gender-affirming surgeries (Schillace 2021). And by 1929, Germany was on the brink of repealing a longstanding anti-sodomy law (Beachy 2014: Chapter 8). Then the country descended into fascism and the Nazi regime banned gay and lesbian organizations. They raided the Institute for Sexual Research, burning tens of thousands of books, journals, and irreplaceable research materials. They revised the anti-sodomy law to criminalize homosexuality more broadly and, under this law, arrested more than 100,000 men (United States Holocaust Memorial Museum 2021; Whisnant 2016).

Amid the current wave of democratic erosion, LGBTQ+ rights are again under threat. Efforts to roll back LGBTQ+ rights in the US have skyrocketed, with state legislatures introducing *hundreds* of anti-LGBTQ+ bills in 2024 (Factora 2024). In 2021, the Hungarian parliament passed a new law that, among other things, prohibits TV stations from showing content that "popularizes" LGBTQ+ identities between 5am and 10pm (Novak 2021). In 2018, Brazil elected as President a man who said he would rather have a dead son than a gay son (Sobel 2018). Even in countries that have so far fended off major threats to their democratic institutions, attacks on LGBTQ+ communities have often gained traction. The United Kingdom has "gone backwards" over the last decade, with "anti-trans hatred [...] widespread in the media and government agendas" (TGEU 2023); trans people in the UK today are subject to widespread discrimination and systematic denials of access to healthcare.

Should we take these examples as an indication that the progress we have seen in Latin America is fragile, liable to be undone in an instant? Returning to the case of Argentina, recent events point to a rising right-wing threat, but also encouraging signs of pushback from a society that has grown far more accepting in recent decades.

Throughout this text, Argentina has emerged as a notable success story. In 1984, only *ten percent* of Argentines believed that homosexuality could be "justified." Today, approximately three-quarters of Argentines support same-sex marriage and equal rights for trans people. In the early 21st century, Argentina emerged as a pioneer in LGBTQ+ rights: in 2010, becoming the first Latin American country to legalize same-sex marriage, and in 2012, passing the most progressive gender identity law in the world.

Yet for all the success that Argentina has had in building a more inclusive and accepting society, recent events highlight that LGBTQ+ rights and protections must be continually defended. In August 2024, the newly elected President Javier Milei's government officially shut down the country's anti-discrimination agency (*Instituto Nacional contra la Discriminación, la Xenofobia y el Racismo*, or INADI). The agency managed thousands of complaints each year, many involving discrimination on the basis of gender and sexual orientation, and it played a key role in passing the 2012 Gender Identity Law.

Milei's government has promoted a clear anti-LGBTQ+ rights agenda, with a goal of eliminating anything they define as "gender ideology." The administration defunded a phone line responsible for supporting victims of gender-based violence, and dramatically reduced the budget across the board for gender-related issues (Iglesias 2024). Milei has stated that one of the goals of his government is to roll back key provisions of Argentina's groundbreaking Gender Identity Law. In February, 2025, Milei passed a decree that banned gender-affirming care for trans youth – putting Argentine policy at odds with a widespread international medical consensus (Booth 2025).

Some of the threats are, for the time being, rhetoric, not policy. Though we would caution against understating the importance of rhetoric as a political action: what begins as elite rhetoric often paves the way for eventual policy changes, even if those changes are years down the road. Elite rhetoric can gradually shift perceptions of what is possible and what is acceptable. And as many citizens in the United States recently learned in the first months of Trump's second administration: when a politician says they will roll back fundamental rights or dismantle key governmental functions, it is a dangerous gamble to assume that it's "just talk" and won't actually be realized.

But even in light of threats and setbacks in Argentina, important lessons can be gleaned from the country's successes. Even as the Argentine electorate sent a far-right politician to the *Casa Rosada*, the people continue to express support for LGBTQ+ rights. In a May 2024 survey, 72% of respondents said they support marriage equality and 70% anti-discrimination policies for transgender people.[46]

One encouraging sign on the durability of LGBTQ+ support comes from an event held in May 2024 to market a new biography of Milei, *Milei: La revolución que no vieron venir* (Milei: The revolution they didn't see coming). The event was promoted with great fanfare. Expecting some 2,000 attendees, they had relocated to a larger auditorium to accommodate the anticipated audience.

---

[46] Encuesta de satisfacción política y opinión pública, May 2024, Universidad de San Andrés.

One of the authors, Nicolás Marquez, had appeared on a radio program the week before. During the interview, he said "There are objectively healthy behaviors and objectively unhealthy behaviors. When the State promotes, encourages, and finances homosexuality – as it has done until Javier Milei appeared on the scene – it is encouraging self-destructive behavior."[47]

Marquez faced strong repudiation after his comments. And when he showed up to present his new book, he faced protesters outside, shouting *"eso no es libertad, eso es odio"* ("that's not freedom, that's hate"). And inside, he found himself speaking to a mostly empty room.[48]

Around the world, many of today's attacks focus on trans rights, with opponents leveraging the fact that public opinion is less well-developed on these issues. If this book provides one key lesson for resisting these attacks, it is that durable progress requires highlighting and communicating the humanity of minority groups: from personal interactions to positive media portrayals to framing the politics around human rights, creating opportunities for empathy is one of the most effective tools to fight back against efforts to dehumanize and repress.

In the presence of widespread public support for LGBTQ+ rights, it becomes much more difficult for politicians to roll back those rights. Just as public opinion on LGBTQ+ rights acted as a constraint in the fight to legalize same-sex marriage, it also constrains politicians' abilities to roll back those rights. Building a more tolerant society and establishing legal protections creates at least a partially self-reinforcing equilibrium.

---

[47] Translated from: "Hay conductas objetivamente sanas y conductas objetivamente insanas. Cuando el Estado promueve, incentiva y financia la homosexualidad – como lo ha hecho hasta la aparición de Javier Milei en escena – está incentivando una conducta autodestructiva." Quoted in Página (2024).

[48] See the MinutoUno (2024) article titled "To an empty room: the libertarians Nicolás Marquez y Agustín Laje presented their book on Javier Milei and no one was there" (translated from *A sala vacía: los libertarios Nicolás Marquez y Agustín Laje presentaron el libro de Javier Milei y no fue nadie*).

References

Adamczyk, A., & Pitt, C. (2009). Shaping Attitudes about Homosexuality: The Role of Religion and Cultural Context. *Social Science Research*, *38*(2): 338–351.

Aksoy, C. G., Carpenter, C. S., De Haas, R., & Tran, K. D. (2020). Do Laws Shape Attitudes? Evidence from same-Sex Relationship Recognition Policies in Europe. *European Economic Review*, *124*: 103399.

Allport, G. W. (1954). *The Nature of Prejudice. Addison-Wesley google schola*, *2*, 59–82.

América TV. (2021). *Gerardo Romano, sobre el beso con Rodolfo Ranni: "Era la primera historia de amor gay en ficción"*.

Angelo, E., & Bain, J. H. (eds.). (1997). *Odysseus: The International Gay Travel Planner*. Port Washington, NY: Odysseus Enterprises.

Armas, D. A., & Mercedes, H. (2022). *Actitudes hacia la homosexualidad en estudiantes del nivel secundario de instituciones educativas de los distritos de Víctor Larco y el Porvenir* (Unpublished doctoral dissertation). Universidad Cesar Vallejo, Peru.

Arriagada, I. (2006). Changes and Inequality in Latin American Families. *Journal of Comparative Family Studies*, *37*(4): 511–537.

Ayoub, P. M., & Garretson, J. (2017). Getting the Message Out: Media Context and Global Changes in Attitudes Toward Homosexuality. *Comparative Political Studies*, *50*(8): 1055–1085.

Bazán, O. (2006). *Historia de la homosexualidad en la Argentina: de la conquista de América al siglo XXI*. Buenos Aires: Marea Editorial.

Beachy, R. (2014). *Gay Berlin: Birthplace of a Modern Identity*. New York: Knopf Doubleday Publishing Group.

Bellucci, M. (2010). *Orgullo: Carlos Jáuregui, una biografía política*. Buenos Aires: Emecé.

Ben, P., & Insausti, S. J. (2021). Historical Trends Leading to the Same-Sex Marriage Law in Argentina. *Cahiers des Amériques latines*, (98): 153–169.

Bimbi, B. (2011). *Matrimonio igualitario*. Buenos Aires: Grupo Planeta – Argentina.

Bimbi, B. (2017). *El fin del armario. Lesbianas, gays, bisexuales y trans en el siglo XXI*. Buenos Aires: Marea Editorial.

Bishin, B. G., Hayes, T. J., Incantalupo, M. B., & Smith, C. A. (2016). Opinion Backlash and Public Attitudes: Are Political Advances in Gay Rights Counterproductive? *American Journal of Political Science*, *60*(3): 625–648.

Boas, T. C. (2020). The Electoral Representation of Evangelicals in Latin America. In Oxford Research Encyclopedia of Politics. Retrieved 10 Oct. 2025, from https://oxfordre.com/politics/view/10.1093/acrefore/9780190228637.001.0001/acrefore-9780190228637-e-1748.

Booth, A. (2025). Advocates Condemn Decree Restricting Treatment for Trans Children in Argentina *Buenos Aires Herald*.

Botero, S. (2022). Working in New Political Spaces: The Checkered History of Latin American Judicialization. In S. Botero, D. M. Brinks, & E. A. Gonzalez-Ocantos (eds.), *The Limits of Judicialization* (pp. 1–38). Cambridge: Cambridge University Press.

Bramlett, B. H. (2012). The Cross-Pressures of Religion and Contact with Gays and Lesbians, and Their Impact on Same-Sex Marriage Opinion. *Politics & Policy*, 40(1): 13–42.

Broockman, D., & Kalla, J. (2016). Durably Reducing Transphobia: A Field Experiment on Door-to-Door Canvassing. *Science*, 352(6282): 220–224.

Brown, R., & Hewstone, M. (2005). An Integrative Theory of Intergroup Contact. In M. P. Zanna (Ed.), *Advances in experimental social psychology*, Vol. 37, pp. 255–343). Elsevier Academic Press. https://doi.org/10.1016/S0065-2601(05)37005-5.

Casas, L. (2009). Invoking Conscientious Objection in Reproductive Health Care: Evolving Issues in Peru, Mexico and Chile. *Reproductive Health Matters*, 17(34): 78–87.

Castorena, O., Rau, E., Schweizer-Robinson, V., & Zechmeister, E. J. (2024). *LGBTQ+ Tolerance in Latin America and the Caribbean*. (LAPOP Working Paper.)

Chaux, E., & León, M. (2016). Homophobic Attitudes and Associated Factors among Adolescents: A Comparison of Six Latin American Countries. *Journal of Homosexuality*, 63(9): 1253–1276.

Chaux, E., León, M., Cuellar, L., & Martínez, J. (2021). Public Opinion toward LGBT People and Rights in Latin America and the Caribbean. In *Oxford Research Encyclopedia of Politics*. Oxford University Press.

Coppari, N., Arcondo, G., Bagnoli, L., Chaves, M., Corvalán, M., Enciso, A. Melgarejo, K., and Rodríguez, X. (2014). Prejuicio y distancia social hacia la homosexualidad en universitarios de psicología de Paraguay. *Salud & Sociedad*, 5(3): 240–252.

Cordero, P. A. M. (2018). *Índice de tolerancia a las diversidades sexuales en estudiantes universitarios de la ciudad de Cuenca* (Unpublished doctoral dissertation). Universidad del Azuay, Ecuador.

Corrales, J. (2021). *The Politics of LGBTQ Rights Expansion in Latin America and the Caribbean*. New York: Cambridge University Press.

Corrales, J., & Pecheny, M. (eds.). (2010). *The Politics of Sexuality in Latin America: A Reader on Lesbian, Gay, Bisexual, and Transgender Rights*. Pittsburgh, PA: University of Pittsburgh Press.

Cuesta, L., & Reynolds, S. (2022). Testing the Economic Independence Hypothesis: Union Formation among Single Mothers in Chile. *Journal of Family Issues*, *43*(1): 96–123.

Daby, M., & Moseley, M. W. (2024). *Mobilizing for Abortion Rights in Latin America* (Cambridge Elements ed.). New York: Cambridge University Press.

de Abreu Maia, L., Chiu, A., & Desposato, S. (2023). No Evidence of Backlash: LGBT Rights in Latin America. *The Journal of Politics*, *85*(1): 49–63.

De Paulo, A. (2017). "Cris Miró les abrió las puertas a todas las que siguieron". Diario Popular. www.diariopopular.com.ar/espectaculos/cris-miro-les-abrio-las-puertas-todas-las-que-siguieron-n278066.

Díez, J., & Dion, M. L. (2018). New Media and Support for Same-Sex Marriage. *Latin American Research Review*, *53*(3): 466–484.

Dion, M. L., & Díez, J. (2017). Democratic Values, Religiosity, and Support for Same-Sex Marriage in Latin America. *Latin American Politics and Society*, *59*(4): 75–98.

Dion, M. L., & Díez, J. (2022). Social Contact with Same-Sex Married Couples and Support for Marriage Equality: Evidence from Argentina. *Politics, Groups, and Identities*, *10*(2): 315–333.

Dyck, J. J., & Pearson-Merkowitz, S. (2012). The Conspiracy of Silence: Context and Voting on Gay Marriage Ballot Measures. *Political Research Quarterly*, *65*(4): 745–757.

Encarnación, O. G. (2011). Latin America's Gay Rights Revolution. *Journal of Democracy*, *22*(2):104–118.

Encarnación, O. G. (2016). *Out in the Periphery: Latin America's Gay Rights Revolution*. New York: Oxford University Press.

Encarnación, O. G. (2018). A Latin American Puzzle: Gay Rights Landscapes in Argentina and Brazil. *Human Rights Quarterly*, *40*(1): 194–218.

Entman, R. M., & Rojecki, A. (2001). The Black Image in the White Mind: Media and Race in America. Chicago: University of Chicago Press.

Esteve, A., Lesthaeghe, R., & López-Gay, A. (2012). The Latin American Cohabitation Boom, 1970–2007. *Population and Development Review*, *38*(1): 55–81.

Factora, J. (2024). A Terrifying 300 Anti-LGBTQ+ Bills Have Already Been Introduced in 2024. www.them.us/story/300-anti-lgbtq-bills-state-legislatures-aclu.

Fernández de Kirchner, C. (2010). Palabras de la Presidenta en acto de promulgación Ley Matrimonio Igualitario. Casa Rosada Presidencia. www.casarosada.gob.ar/informacion/archivo/22424-blank-63939869

Fernández de Kirchner, C. (2019). *Sinceramente.* Buenos Aires: Penguin Random House Grupo Editorial Argentina.

Firebaugh, G., & Davis, K. E. (1988). Trends in Antiblack Prejudice, 1972–1984: Region and Cohort Effects. *American Journal of Sociology*, 94(2): 251–272.

Flores, A. R. (2015). Attitudes toward Transgender Rights: Perceived Knowledge and Secondary Interpersonal Contact. *Politics, Groups, and Identities*, 3(3): 398–416.

Flores, A. R., & Barclay, S. (2016). Backlash, Consensus, Legitimacy, or Polarization: The Effect of Same-Sex Marriage Policy on Mass Attitudes. *Political Research Quarterly*, 69(1): 43–56.

Fullam, L. (2015). *"Gender Theory," Nuclear War, and the Nazis / Commonweal Magazine.* www.commonwealmagazine.org/gender-theory-nuclear-war-and-nazis-0.

García, B., & Rojas, O. (2001). Recent Transformations in Latin American Families: A Socio-Demographic Perspective. Paper presented at the XXIV General Population Conference of IUSSP. Session S45 "The Demography of Latin America", organized by José Miguel Guzmán.

Garretson, J. J. (2015). Exposure to the Lives of Lesbians and Gays and the Origin of Young People's Greater Support for Gay Rights. *International Journal of Public Opinion Research*, 27(2): 277–288.

Gmünder, B. (2000). *Spartacus: international gay guide 2000/2001.* Berlin: Bruno Gmunder. https://archive.org/details/spartacusinterna0000gmun_29 thedi.

Gomes, S. D. S. R., & Cantu, R. (2023). The Conservative Wave and Corporate Practices in Brazil: The Controversy over LGBTQ in Marketing. *Journal of Latin American Studies*, 55(2): 267–292.

González, M. A. (2008). Latinos ACT UP: Transnational AIDS Activism in the 1990s. *NACLA Report on the Americas*, 41(4): 35–39.

Gonzalez-Ocantos, E. A. (2019). *The Politics of Transitional Justice in Latin America: Power, Norms, and Capacity Building* (1st ed.). New York: Cambridge University Press.

González-Rostani, V., & Morgenstern, S. (2023). Legislators' Religiosity and Same-Sex Marriage in Latin America. *Latin American Research Review*, 58(3): 539–560.

Greene, K., Rossiter, E., Seira, E., & Simpser, A. (2024). Interacting as Equals: How Contact Can Promote Tolerance among Opposing Partisans. *Nature Human Behavior*, 9(1): 147–155. doi: https://doi.org/10.1038/s41562-024-02043-y.

Guiñazú, G. (2024). *Zona de riesgo: la historia detrás del programa en el que dos hombres se besaron por primera vez y cambió la televisión argentina*. Clarín, online, accessed 9/29/24. URL: www.clarin.com/espectaculos/zona-riesgo-historia-detras-programa-hombres-besaron-primera-vez-cambio-television-argentina_0_g0SwAXMIvc.html.

Gulesci, S., Lombardi, M., & Ramos, A. (2024). Telenovelas and Attitudes toward the LGBTQ+ Community in Latin America. *Labour Economics*, 87: 102488.

Heger, H. (1994). *The Men with the Pink Triangle: The True, Life- and-Death Story of Homosexuals in the Nazi Death Camps*. Boston: Alyson Publications.

Herek, G. M., & Capitanio, J. P. (1996). "Some of My Best Friends": Intergroup Contact, Concealable Stigma, and Heterosexuals' Attitudes Toward Gay Men and Lesbians. *Personality and Social Psychology Bulletin*, 22(4): 412–424.

Herek, G. M., & Glunt, E. K. (1993). Interpersonal Contact and Heterosexuals' Attitudes toward Gay Men: Results from a National Survey. *Journal of Sex Research*, 30(3): 239–244.

Hiller, R. (2017). *Conyugalidad y ciudadanía*. Buenos Aires: Teseo.

Hoffman, M. L. (2000). *Empathy and Moral Development: Implications for Caring and Justice*. Cambridge: Cambridge University Press.

Horton, D., & Richard Wohl, R. (1956). Mass Communication and Parasocial Interaction: Observations on Intimacy at a Distance. *Psychiatry*, 19(3): 215–229.

Htun, M. (2003). *Sex and the State: Abortion, Divorce and the Family under Latin American Dictatorships and Democracies*. Cambridge: Cambridge University Press.

Hummel, C., & Velasco-Guachalla, V. (2024). Activists, Parties, and the Expansion of Trans Rights in Bolivia. *Comparative Politics*, 56(3): 321–343.

Iglesias, M. (2024). Milei y las mujeres: las quiere sin jubilación y lejos de la Corte Suprema. *Clarín*. Online, accessed 4/18/25. URL: www.clarin.com/opinion/milei-mujeres-quiere-jubilacion-lejos-corte-suprema_0_2zu1Nz25M0.html?srsltid=AfmBOoqVOECvvgwWhVdOxYapx0PmrPS60CFjKH4GuKOD0l4cy8psdb4c.

Insausti, S. J., & Ben, P. (2023). Homonationalism, LGBT Desaparecidos, and the Politics of Queer Memory in Argentina. *Memory Studies*, 16(1): 66–84.

Jones, P. E. (2022). Respectability Politics and Straight Support for LGB Rights. *Political Research Quarterly*, *75*(4): 935–949.

Jones, P. E., Brewer, P. R., Young, D. G., Lambe, J. L., & Hoffman, L. H. (2018). Explaining Public Opinion toward Transgender People, Rights, and Candidates. *Public Opinion Quarterly*, *82*(2): 252–278.

Jung, J.- H., & Tavits, M. (2024). *Counter-Stereotypes and Attitudes Toward Gender and LGBTQ Equality* (1st ed.). Cambridge University Press.

Junior, G., & Gonçalves, N. (2017). GLBT Character Design in Telenovelas: Approaches to the complex issue of Inclusion. *DIS (ISSN: 2594-2336), Vol 1, Núm. 1 (2017), julio - diciembre, pp. 114–124*.

Kalla, J. L., & Broockman, D. E. (2020). Reducing Exclusionary Attitudes through Interpersonal Conversation: Evidence from Three Field Experiments. *American Political Science Review*, *114*(2): 410–425.

Keck, M. E., & Sikkink, K. (1998). *Activists beyond Borders*. Ithaca, NY: Cornell University Press.

Kenny, C., & Patel, D. (2017). *Norms and Reform: Legalizing Homosexuality Improves Attitudes* [SSRN Scholarly Paper]. Rochester, NY.

Knox, D. (2023). *Pope Francis Calls for the Inclusion of Trans People in Catholic Church Practices - GLAAD*. https://glaad.org/pope-francis-calls-for-the-inclusion-of-trans-people-in-catholic-practices/.

Küng, S. A., Wilkins, J. D., de León, F. D., Huaraz, F., & Pearson, E. (2021). "We don't want problems": reasons for denial of legal abortion based on conscientious objection in Mexico and Bolivia. *Reproductive Health*, *18*(1): 44.

Lamond, I. R. (2018). The challenge of articulating human rights at an LGBT 'mega-event': a personal reflection on Sao Paulo Pride 2017. *Leisure Studies*, *37*(1): 36–48.

Lewin, M., & Wornat, O. (2020). *Putas y guerrilleras*. Buenos Aires, Argentina: Planeta.

Lewis, G. B. (2011). The Friends and Family Plan: Contact with Gays and Support for Gay Rights. *Policy Studies Journal*, *39*(2): 217–238.

Lipsky, B. (2021). *Carlos Jáuregui: 'Pride Is a Political Response'*.

Lodola, G., & Corral, M. (2010). Support for Same-Sex Marriage in Latin America. *Americas Barometer Insights*, (2010) 44. www.vanderbilt.edu/lapop/insights/I0844.enrevised.pdf.

Malta, M., Cardoso, R., Montenegro, L., De Jesus, J. G., Seixas, M., Benevides, B., . . . Whetten, K. (2019). Sexual and gender minorities rights in Latin America and the Caribbean: A multi-country evaluation. *BMC International Health and Human Rights*, *19*(1): 31.

Mansilla, G. (2014). *Yo nena, yo princesa*. Argentina: Ediciones UNGS.

McGee, M. J., & Kampwirth, K. (2015). The Co-optation of LGBT Movements in Mexico and Nicaragua: Modernizing Clientelism? *Latin American Politics and Society*, *57*(4): 51–73.

MinutoUno. (2024). *A sala vacía: los libertarios Nicolás Marquez y Agustín Laje presentaron el libro de Javier Milei y no fue nadie.*

Moscowitz, L. (2013). *The battle over marriage: Gay rights activism through the media.* Champaign, IL: University of Illinois Press.

Negretto, G. L. (2013). *Making Constitutions: Presidents, Parties, and Institutional Choice in Latin America.* Cambridge: Cambridge University Press.

Norton, A. T., & Herek, G. M. (2013). Heterosexuals' Attitudes Toward Transgender People: Findings from a National Probability Sample of U.S. Adults. *Sex Roles*, *68*(11–12): 738–753.

Novak, B. (2021). Hungary Adopts Child Sex Abuse Law That Also Targets L.G.B.T. Community. *The New York Times.*

O'Donnell, G. A., & Schmitter, P. C. (1986). *Transitions from Authoritarian Rule: Tentative Conclusions about Uncertain Democracies.* Baltimore: Johns Hopkins University Press.

Ofosu, E. K., Chambers, M. K., Chen, J. M., & Hehman, E. (2019). Same-sex marriage legalization associated with reduced implicit and explicit antigay bias. *Proceedings of the National Academy of Sciences*, *116*(18): 8846–8851.

Ordóñez, L. B. C., Bulla, L. C. T., Guzmán, K. P., & Céspedes, A. L. P. (2017). Representaciones sociales de adolescentes sobre la homosexualidad, el matrimonio entre personas del mismo sexo y la adopción homoparental. *Revista del Centro Reina Sofía sobre Adolescencia y Juventud*, (6): 76–96.

Osorio, J. M. P. (2014). Estudiantes universitarios ante la diversidad. Significados del homosexual. *Psicología para América Latina*, (27): 66–92.

Otero Galindo, M. D. P., & Meertens, D. J. (2020). *La discriminación una forma constante de vulneración de derechos para la población LGBT de Bogotá* (Unpublished doctoral dissertation). Pontificia Universidad Javeriana.

Paradela-López, M., Antón, J.- I., & Jima-González, A. (2023). How Much Have We Changed? Long-Term Determinants of Attitudes toward Homosexuality in Chile. *Latin American Research Review*, *58*(3): 575–594.

Pettigrew, T. F. (1998). Intergroup Contact Theory. *Annual Review of Psychology*, *49*(Volume 49, 1998): 65–85.

Pettigrew, T. F., & Tropp, L. R. (2006). A meta-analytic test of intergroup contact theory. *Journal of Personality and Social Psychology*, *90*(5): 751–783.

Prothro, J. W., & Grigg, C. M. (1960). Fundamental Principles of Democracy: Bases of Agreement and Disagreement. *The Journal of Politics*, *22*(2): 276–294.

Przeworski, A. (1991). *Democracy and the Market.* New York, NY: Cambridge University Press.

Puenzo, L. (2007). *XXY.* Distribution Company.

Puenzo, L. (2009). *The fish child.* Wanda Vision.

Página. (2024). *El biógrafo de Milei presentó su libro ante un auditorio semivacío / En la Feria del Libro.*

Ramm, A. (2016). Changing Patterns of Kinship: Cohabitation, Patriarchy and Social Policy in Chile. *Journal of Latin American Studies, 48*(4): 769–796.

Reuters. (2024). *Pope Francis calls for studies into 'ugly' gender theory/ Reuters.*

Salinas, V. (2011). Socioeconomic Differences According to Family Arrangements in Chile. *Population Research and Policy Review, 30*(5): 677–699.

Samuels, D. (2004). From Socialism to Social Democracy: Party Organization and the Transformation of the Workers' Party in Brazil. *Comparative Political Studies, 37*(9): 999–1024.

Schiappa, E., Gregg, P. B., & Hewes, D. E. (2006). Can one TV show make a difference? Will & Grace and the Parasocial Contact Hypothesis. *Journal of Homosexuality, 51*(4): 15–37.

Schillace, B. (2021). *The Forgotten History of the World's First Trans Clinic.*

Seligson, M., Morales, D. E. M., & Russo, G. A. (2019). Education, the wealth of nations, and political tolerance toward homosexuals: a multilevel analysis of 26 countries in the Americas. *Opinião Pública, 25*(2): 234–257.

Sikkink, K. (2011). *The Justice Cascade.* New York, NY: W. W. Norton & Company, Inc.

Skipworth, S. A., Garner, A., & Dettrey, B. J. (2010). Limitations of the Contact Hypothesis: Heterogeneity in the Contact Effect on Attitudes toward Gay Rights. *Politics & Policy, 38*(5): 887–906.

Smith, A. E., & Boas, T. C. (2023). Religion, Sexuality Politics, and the Transformation of Latin American Electorates. *British Journal of Political Science*, 1–20. doi:10.1017/S0007123423000613.

Sobel, A. (2018). *Brazil's Presidential Front-Runner: Rather Have My Son Dead Than Gay.*

Sosa Villada, C. (2019). *Las malas.* Buenos Aires, Argentina: Tusquets Editores.

Tankard, M. E., & Paluck, E. L. (2017). The effect of a Supreme Court decision regarding gay marriage on social norms and personal attitudes. *Psychological science, 28*(9): 1334–1344.

Tate, J. (2013). Redefining Mexican Masculinity in Twenty-First Century Telenovelas. *Hispanic Research Journal, 14*(6): 538–552.

TGEU. (2023). *10 Years of Trans Rights Mapping in Europe & Central Asia: Decade-long Research Reveals Overall Progress, While UK & Hungary Go Backwards.*

The Economist. (2023). Latin America's single mothers are being left behind. *The Economist.*

Undurraga, V., & Sadler, M. (2019). The misrepresentation of conscientious objection as a new strategy of resistance to abortion decriminalisation. *Sexual and Reproductive Health Matters, 27*(2): 17–19.

United Nations. (1995). *Declaration of Principles on Tolerance.* www.unesco.org/en/legal-affairs/declaration-principles-tolerance

United States Holocaust Memorial Museum. (2021). *Paragraph 175.*

van Quaquebeke, N., Henrich, D. C., & Eckloff, T. (2007). "It's not tolerance I'm asking for, it's respect!" A conceptual framework to differentiate between tolerance, acceptance and (two types of) respect. *Gruppe. Interaktion. Organisation. Zeitschrift für Angewandte Organisationspsychologie (GIO), 38*(2): 185–200.

Verkuyten, M., Yogeeswaran, K., & Adelman, L. (2020). The Negative Implications of Being Tolerated: Tolerance From the Target's Perspective. *Perspectives on Psychological Science, 15*(3): 544–561.

Wedeen, L. (2009). *Ambiguities of Domination: Politics, Rhetoric, and Symbols in Contemporary Syria* (t. Author, Ed.). Chicago, IL: University of Chicago Press.

Whisnant, C. J. (2016). *Queer Identities and Politics in Germany: A History, 1880–1945.* Columbia University Press.

Williamson, M. (2024). A Global Analysis of Transgender Rights: Introducing the Trans Rights Indicator Project (TRIP). *Perspectives on Politics, 22*(3): 799–818.

Winfield, N., & Thomas, T. (2023). *For this group of trans women, the pope and his message of inclusivity are a welcome change.* https://apnews.com/article/vatican-transgender-lgbtq-b3d67868504ba701cce09da9ecc94de0.

Zaremberg, G., & Almeida, D. R. d. (2022). *Feminisms in Latin America: Prochoice Nested Networks in Mexico and Brazil.* Cambridge University Press.

Cambridge Elements

Gender and Politics

Tiffany D. Barnes
University of Texas at Austin

Tiffany D. Barnes is Professor of Political Science at the University of Texas at Austin. She is the author of *Women, Politics, and Power: A Global Perspective* (Rowman & Littlefield, 2007) and the award-winning *Gendering Legislative Behavior* (Cambridge University Press, 2016). Her research has been funded by the National Science Foundation (NSF) and recognized with numerous awards. Barnes is the former president of the MidwestWomen's Caucus and founder and director of the Empirical Study of Gender (EGEN) network.

Diana Z. O'Brien
Washington University in St. Louis

Diana Z. O'Brien is the Bela Kornitzer Distinguished Professor of Political Science at Washington University in St. Louis. She specializes in the causes and consequences of women's political representation. Her award-winning research has been supported by the NSF and published in leading political science journals. O'Brien has also served as a Fulbright Visiting Professor, an associate editor at *Politics & Gender*, the president of the Midwest Women's Caucus, and a founding member of the EGEN network.

About the Series

From campaigns and elections to policymaking and political conflict, gender pervades every facet of politics. Elements in Gender and Politics features carefully theorized, empirically rigorous scholarship on gender and politics. The Elements both offer new perspectives on foundational questions in the field and identify and address emerging research areas.

Cambridge Elements =

Gender and Politics

Elements in the Series

In Love and at War: Marriage in Non-state Armed Groups
Hilary Matfess

Counter-Stereotypes and Attitudes Toward Gender and LGBTQ Equality
Jae-Hee Jung and Margit Tavits

The Politics of Bathroom Access and Exclusion in the United States
Sara Chatfield

Women, Gender, and Rebel Governance during Civil Wars
Meredith Maloof Loken

Abortion Attitudes and Polarization in the American Electorate
Erin C. Cassese, Heather L. Ondercin and Jordan Randall

Gender, Ethnicity, and Intersectionality in Cabinets: Asia and Europe in Comparative Perspective
Amy H. Liu, Roman Hlatky, Keith Padraic Chew, Eoin L. Power, Sam Selsky, Betty Compton and Meiying Xu

Gendered Jobs and Local Leaders: Women, Work, and the Pipeline to Local Political Office
Rachel Bernhard and Mirya R. Holman

What's Happened to the Gender Gap in Political Activity?: Social Structure, Politics, and Participation in the United States
Shauna L. Shames, Sara Morell, Ashley Jardina, Kay Lehman Schlozman and Nancy Burns

Family Matters: How Romantic Partners Shape Politicians' Careers
Olle Folke, Moa Frödin Gruneau and Johanna Rickne

Glass Ceilings, Glass Cliffs, and Quicksands: Gendered Party Leadership in Parliamentary Systems
Andrea S. Aldrich and Zeynep Somer-Topcu

Attitudes toward Political Authoritarianism in Economically Advanced Democracies: The Role of Gender Values and Norms
Amy C. Alexander and Gefjon Off

Towards Tolerance and Acceptance: Public Opinion and LGBTQ+ Politics in Latin America
Mariela Daby and Eli G. Rau

A full series listing is available at: www.cambridge.org/EGAP

For EU product safety concerns, contact us at Calle de José Abascal, 56–1°,
28003 Madrid, Spain or eugpsr@cambridge.org.

www.ingramcontent.com/pod-product-compliance
Ingram Content Group UK Ltd.
Pitfield, Milton Keynes, MK11 3LW, UK
UKHW022118130426
469895UK00018B/295